Step by Step Exchange 2007 to 2010 Migration

The Work Book Series

Start to End Detailed Step by Step process in as it happens in real life sequences of Migrating your Microsoft Exchange Server from version 2007 to 2010.

Chetan Pawar

Contents

COLLECTING INFORMATION ABOUT YOUR EXISTING EXCHANGE SERVER 2007 ENVIRONMENT

A successful migration to Exchange Server 2010 depends a lot on your understanding of the existing Exchange Server 2007 environment.

There are many pieces of information that you should collect before you can begin installing Exchange Server 2010. Some of these will be collected by using software tools, while others must be collected manually through inspection of the current servers or speaking with other people in the organization.

As you progress through this section you can use the planning worksheet that is included with this guide to record the information that you collect.

RUNNING THE EXCHANGE PROFILE ANALYZER

The Exchange Profile Analyzer is used to collect statistical information about the Exchange organization that is helpful for understanding the size and makeup of the Exchange data that is to be migrated.

Install the Exchange Profile Analyzer by running the setup MSI file you downloaded earlier. For this demonstration I am installing the Exchange Profile Analyzer on the head office domain controller, HE-DC.

The Exchange Profile Analyzer will need an account to perform its analysis of the Exchange environment. The account should be delegated **Exchange View-Only Administrator** rights only, and can't be a member of **Domain Admins** or **Enterprise Admins**.

In this example I have created a domain user account named "epa" (*please remember; don't make the account a Domain Admin or Enterprise Admin*). Then on an existing Exchange Server 2007 server launch the Exchange Management Shell and run the **Add-ExchangeAdministrator** command.

```
[PS] C:\>Add-ExchangeAdministrator -Identity epa -Role ViewOnlyAdmin
```

Next, use the **Add-ADPermission** command to grant the account Send-As and Receive-As rights on each existing Exchange 2007 Mailbox server.

```
[PS] C:\> Get-ExchangeServer HO-EX2007-MB1 | Add-ADPermission -user epa -AccessRights
extendedright -ExtendedRights "send-as"
[PS] C:\> Get-ExchangeServer HO-EX2007-PF1 | Add-ADPermission -user epa -AccessRights
extendedright -ExtendedRights "receive-as"
[PS] C:\> Get-ExchangeServer BR-EX2007-MB | Add-ADPermission -user epa -AccessRights
extendedright -ExtendedRights "receive-as"
```

Launch the Exchange Profile Analyzer from the Start Menu > Microsoft Exchange > Exchange Server Profile Analyser.

When the tool has launched click on **Connect to Active Directory**.

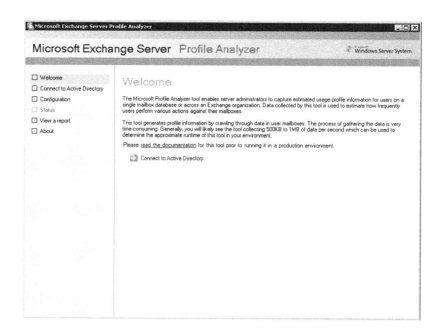

The Profile Analyzer will choose a domain controller by default. You can choose another one if you wish.

Un-tick the **Current User** checkbox and enter the "epa" user credentials.

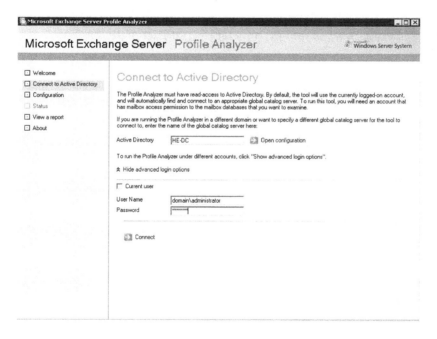

Click on **Connect** to continue. If an error appears that the topology can't be loaded you may not have the account permissions configured correctly, or you may need to wait for replication of the permissions changes to occur before trying again.

Configure the scan options. In the demonstration I am going for the most detailed analysis possibly by including individual mailbox information, and by not specifying a date range for the analysis.

Depending on the size of your environment you may need to use a less aggressive analysis. It is also recommended that you do not start the analysis during normal business hours for your environment.

The Exchange Profile Analyzer will progress at a rate of about 500 kilobytes per second, so the total time taken to perform the analysis will depend on how large your Exchange databases are.

When you're ready to proceed with the scan click on **Start Collect**.

If the collection processes fails validation for one or more mailbox servers, double-check that you have set up the permissions correctly. You may then just need to wait for the changes to fully replicate through your environment.

After the Exchange Profile Analyzer has completed its data collection click on **View Report** to see the results.

Some examples of all the useful information that the Exchange Profile Analyzer will tell you about for your Exchange Server 2010 deployment project planning are listed as below.

Mailbox size statistics let you know the average and largest mailbox sizes in the organization, as well as the total number of mailboxes and total data size.

All sizes are displayed in kilobytes (KB).

Results without Time Frame Applied

⊟ **Mailbox**

Aggregate of mailbox size:	avg:	142,565.76
	min:	0
	max:	3,286,446.00

Total count:	417
Total size:	59,449,924.00

System folder Sizes lets you know whether you can reduce your migration load by purging deleted items or junk mail from mailboxes.

Size of various system folders:

inbox:	31,878,177.00
deleteditems:	1,324,622.00
outbox:	91,117.00
sentitems:	15,522,814.00
journal:	9,963.00
drafts:	154,727.00
junkmail:	44,783.00

Message size statistics lets you know whether most messages in the databases are likely to contain large attachments.

⊟ **Message Size**

Aggregates of message size across all messages:	avg:	76.94
	min:	0
	max:	203,505.02

Number of messages within certain size range:

0 -2:	106804	16.60 %
2-10:	260149	40.44 %
10-100:	221005	34.35 %
100-1024:	46603	7.24 %
1024-5120:	7596	1.18 %
5120-2147483647:	1157	0.18 %

As we see here, the Exchange Profile Analyzer reports contain a lot of useful information that can be used when planning the migration from an Exchange Server 2007 to Exchange Server 2010

IDENTIFYING MAILBOX STORAGE QUOTAS

Most Exchange organizations will have storage quotas configured on the mailbox databases, because unlimited mailbox growth makes capacity planning difficult to maintain.

Exchange Server 2010 mailbox databases have a default storage quota of 2 gigabytes that is quite generous, but you still need to make sure that it is not smaller than what is currently allowed for the Exchange Server 2007 mailbox users.

We can find out the Exchange Server 2007 storage quotas using either the Exchange Management Console or the Exchange Management Shell

In the Exchange Management Console navigate to each mailbox database, then right-click and select Properties. On the Limits tab are the three mailbox storage quota settings.

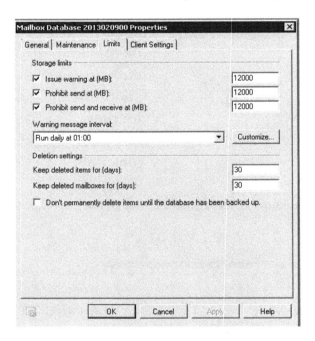

If there are a lot of mailbox databases to inspect then it is easier to use the Exchange Management Shell to retrieve the quota information.

```
[PS] C:\>Get-MailboxDatabase | ft server,name,prohibit*,issue*
Server Name ProhibitSendRec ProhibitSendQuo IssueWarningQuo
eiveQuota ta ta
------ ---- --------------- --------------- ---------------
BR-EX2007-MB Mailbox Data... 2355MB 2GB 1945MB
ho-ex2007-mb1 Mailbox Data... 2355MB 2GB 1945MB
```

IDENTIFYING ROOM AND EQUIPMENT MAILBOXES AND PUBLIC FOLDERS

Exchange Server 2007 and 2010 both have the facility of dedicated mailbox types for managing room and resource scheduling.

These special mailboxes have additional calendar options available for them and can be configured in various ways to suit the business and lower administrative costs, such as by enabling auto-acceptance of bookings.

In Exchange Server 2003 there was only one type of mailbox available and so organizations would have to manually configure calendar permissions, and assign staff or administrators to manage bookings. In other organizations public folder calendars were used instead.

Some organizations continued to use regular user mailboxes even with Exchange Server 2007 introducing Room and Equipment mailboxes

There are two main reasons to identify these resource mailboxes during the planning phase of the project, as follows:
• To take advantage of the new features of Exchange Server 2010 by converting the mailboxes into proper Room and Equipment mailboxes after the mailbox migration is complete
• To understand whether public folders used for resource bookings need to be migrated to Exchange Server 2010

You can quickly list the Room Mailboxes by using the Exchange Management Shell

```
[PS] C:\>Get-Mailbox | where {$_.RecipientTypeDetails -eq "RoomMailbox"}
Name Alias ServerName ProhibitSendQuo
ta
---- ----- ---------- ---------------
BR Meeting Room 1 brmeetingroom1 br-ex2007-mb unlimited
HO Meeting Room 1 homeetingroom1 ho-ex2007-mb1 unlimited
HO Meeting Room 2 homeetingroom2 ho-ex2007-mb1 unlimited
```

But if your organization is using standard user mailboxes for managing rooms and equipment, you may need to manually search for them. If the mailboxes all follow a similar naming standard it might make the task a bit easier.
You should consider converting the mailboxes before migrating to Exchange Server 2010, but it is not essential.

IDENTIFYING PST FILE USAGE

PST files are a legacy hangover from years ago when Exchange servers could not handle large databases, and high speed disk storage was too expensive to allow unrestricted mailbox growth.

Exchange Server 2010 has a highly optimized database format that is designed to perform well for large mailboxes and databases even on relatively low cost disk storage.

This makes it possible to consider importing legacy PST file data back into the Exchange database where it can be properly stored for backup, discover, and more efficient archiving at a later stage. However to do this you need to understand how much PST file data exists in your environment, and be able to plan enough Exchange Server 2010 storage to accommodate it.

IDENTIFYING PUBLIC FOLDER USAGE

Public folders are supported by Exchange Server 2010 however they are not necessarily a requirement.

Microsoft has made it clear that public folders are being deprecated and so organizations that do not need them should not deploy them or begin using them.

In an Exchange Server 2010 environment there are only two reasons to consider retaining public folders:
• You have existing public folder data that is still in use by the business, and can't be migrated to a different platform such as SharePoint
• You have Outlook 2003 clients on the network which require public folders for accessing Free/Busy information

If you have existing public folder databases in your organization it is useful to check for storage limits configured on the databases.
In the Exchange Management Shell run the following command.

```
[PS] C:\>Get-PublicFolderDatabase | ft server,name,prohibit*,issue*,max*
Server Name ProhibitPostQuo IssueWarningQuo MaxItemSize
ta ta
------ ---- --------------- --------------- -----------
HO-EX2007-PF1 Public Folde... 2GB 1945MB 10MB
BR-EX2007-MB Public Folde... 2GB 1945MB 10MB
```

Record the output in the Exchange Migration Worksheet at the end of this book.

IDENTIFYING EMAIL ROUTING TOPOLOGY

Email routing within the Exchange organization is handled by the Active Directory Sites topology, and this unchanged with Exchange Server 2010.

However the routing topology that exists outside of the immediate Exchange organization needs to be understood prior to the migration.

Exchange environments usually use one of the following inbound/outbound email topologies:

• Incoming email is received directly from the internet to a Hub Transport server, and outgoing email is sent out directly to the internet from a Hub Transport server

• Incoming email is received by a smart host (either an on-premise server or a hosted service) and then routed to a Hub Transport server, and outgoing email is sent out again via the smart host.

The smart host may be a third party email security product or appliance, or an ISP hosted mail server. It is important to identify what this server or product is, as well as any firewall access that is required to connect to it, so that the email routing can be changed later on to Exchange Server 2010.

To determine your outbound email route you can use the Exchange Management Shell to list all Send Connectors for the organization.

```
[PS] C:\>Get-SendConnector
Identity AddressSpaces Enabled
-------- ------------- -------
Internet Email Outbound {SMTP:*;1} True
```

Running the same command piped to Format-List will give you more details about whether a smart host is used or not.

```
[PS] C:\>Get-SendConnector | fl
```

For inbound email routing, if a Hub Transport server accepts mail directly from the internet or from a smart host it likely will have its permissions configured to be enabled for Anonymous Users. You can find any Receive Connectors with this configuration by running the following Exchange Management Shell command

```
[PS] C:\>Get-ReceiveConnector | where {$_.PermissionGroups -like "*Anonymous*"}

Identity Bindings Enabled

-------- -------- -------

HO-EX2007-HT1\Default HO-EX2007-HT1 {:::25, 0.0.0.0:25} True
```

If you still aren't sure about the routes that incoming and outgoing emails are taking in your organization you can send some test emails between an internal and external mailbox and then inspect the message headers to determine the path that they took.

Record the details of the Email Topology in the Exchange Migration Worksheet at the end of this book. It is important here to record any non-exchange systems in the topology and their removal methods and steps.

IDENTIFYING CLIENT SOFTWARE VERSIONS

Exchange Server 2010 is compatible with the following Microsoft Outlook versions:
• Outlook 2003 with Service Pack 2
• Outlook 2007
• Outlook 2010

In addition, Exchange Server 2010 may be used by third email clients such as:
• Apple Mail/Entourage
• POP3/IMAP4 clients
Each client version in use on the network should be identified and checked for Exchange Server 2010 compatibility. You should also look for any special configurations that may be required on Exchange Server 2010 to cater for them (e.g. POP3 and IMAP4 are not enabled by default on Exchange Server 2010, and WebDAV is not available at all).

IDENTIFYING MAIL-INTEGRATED APPLICATIONS AND DEVICES

When you migration your organization to Exchange Server 2010 and remove the legacy servers it is very likely to cause a disruption to mail-integrated applications in your network.

To avoid such problems it is recommended that you audit your network for applications or devices that rely on the Exchange servers for their email functionality. These systems may interact with your legacy Exchange using MAPI, IMAP, POP or SMTP.

Examples of mail-integrated systems include:
• Backup servers (for emailed backup reports and notifications)
• Blackberry Enterprise Server (mobile messaging)
• Line of business (e.g. payroll and CRM)
• Telephony systems (e.g. voicemail to email, and presence)
• Microsoft SQL servers
• Third party email signature software
• Antivirus and anti-spam products
• Printers and scanners
• UPS and SAN

In some cases it may be necessary to have discussions with key people within the organization to ask them which applications and systems that they rely on day to day use email in some way.

IDENTIFYING PUBLIC NAMES

The public DNS names used for connecting to Exchange remotely need to be identified so that the configuration of the new Exchange servers, and the migration plan for transitioning to the new servers, are both performed correctly.

Investigate whether your organization uses Exchange remote access methods such as:

• Outlook Web Access

• ActiveSync

• RPC-over-HTTPS

• POP3 or IMAP4

In this guide we'll be using the **mail.chetanpawar.com** public name as an example.

PLANNING FOR SSL CERTIFICATES

Exchange Server 2010 requires HTTPS (SSL) encrypted connections by default for certain remote access services such as Outlook Web App (OWA) and ActiveSync, as well as internal access such as Autodiscover and Exchange Web Services (EWS).

An Exchange Server 2010 server may be configured to answer to several different names, such as:

• The server's fully qualified domain name

- One or more public names such as "mail.exchangeserverpro.net"

- One or more Exchange Web Services names such as "autodiscover.exchangeserverpro.net"

To provide this functionality the Exchange server will need to be configured with a type of SSL certificate known as a Subject Alternative Names (SAN) certificate.
Although SAN certificates were recommended for use with Exchange Server 2007 there were ways to configure servers so that a SAN certificate was not required, so this concept may still be new to some Exchange administrators.

At this planning stage you need to be aware of this SSL requirement, and understand that a new certificate will likely need to be purchased from a commercial Certificate Authority. Although the cost of a few hundred dollars seems expensive, it is less than the time and effort you will spend trying to work around it.

You can use a private Certificate Authority to issue some certificates for internal servers, but that is not recommended for internet-facing servers as it will create certificate trust issues in a lot of situations.

If you want to take a look at your existing SSL certificate (only if one is in use) simply browse to your current Outlook Web Access URL, and in the browser address bar click on the padlock icon.

Click on **View Certificates** to open the certificate. In the **Details** tab of the certificate properties click on the **Subject** field. The information in that field will be useful soon when configuring the new SSL certificate for Exchange Server 2010.

In addition to at least one new SSL certificate for your Exchange Server 2010 servers, you may also need to provision a new SSL certificate for your existing internet-facing Exchange Server 2007 Client Access server (even if it already has one).

This is only necessary if your migration project will involve a gradual migration of mailboxes over a period of days or weeks. This is known as the co-existence period.

During the co-existence period Outlook Web App is published to the Exchange Server 2010 Client Access server, which is configured with a legacy namespace to redirect Exchange Server 2007 mailbox users to the Exchange Server 2007 Client Access server.

The legacy namespace is simply a DNS record that resolves to your internet-facing Exchange Server 2007 Client Access server. It can be any name you like but the convention is to use "legacy", for e.g. legacy.chetanpawar.com.

Because this redirected connection uses SSL it requires that the Exchange Server 2007 includes that legacy name in the SSL certificate configured on the internet-facing Client Access server.

With all of these details in mind there are a few ways you can approach the provisioning of SSL certificates for your Exchange migration project. You can consider:

- Using commercially bought SAN certificates on all Exchange servers

- Using commercially bought SAN certificates only on the internet-facing Exchange servers, and privately issued SAN certificates for the internal servers

• Using privately issued SAN certificates for all servers (not recommended)

Ultimately each Client Access server needs a valid SSL certificate installed with the correct names on it.

Now in this guide we'll be using the following:

• The internet-facing Exchange Server 2007 Client Access server will have a new SSL certificate provisioned that includes the fully-qualified domain name of the server, the public names, as well as the legacy namespace

• The internet-facing Exchange Server 2010 Client Access servers will have a new SSL certificate provisioned that includes the fully-qualified domain names of the servers, as well as the public names

• The branch office Exchange Server 2010 server will have a new SSL certificate provisioned from an internal Certificate Authority that includes the fully-qualified domain name of the server

• The branch office Exchange Server 2007 server does not need any new certificates provisioned

A Migrator must record the existing SSL certificate details including the name on the certificate, the provider, as well as the organization details along with the details of each of the SSL certificates that will be needed to be acquired for the new servers.

PLANNING IP ADDRESSES

Each of the new Exchange Server 2010 servers will need an IP address allocated to it. In addition to the normal server IP addresses you may also need additional IP addresses.

• If you are deploying a Client Access Server array using Windows NLB you will need an additional IP address for each NLB member, as well as at least one IP address for the virtual cluster IP.

• If you are deploying a Database Availability Group you will need at least one IP address to assign to the DAG, and IP addresses for any network interfaces that will be used for a dedicated replication network.

ENVIRONMENT PRE-REQUISITES FOR EXCHANGE SERVER 2010

ACTIVE DIRECTORY PRE-REQUISITES

Active Directory requires the following to support Exchange Server 2010

Component	Requirement
Schema Master	The Schema Master must be running one of the following operating systems: • Windows Server 2003 Standard/Enterprise with SP1 (x86 or x64) • Windows Server 2003 R2 Standard/Enterprise with SP1 (x86 or x64) • Windows Server 2008 Standard/Enterprise (x86 or x64) • Windows Server 2008 R2 Standard/Enterprise
Global Catalog	In each Site that will contain an Exchange server there must be at least one Global Catalog running one of the above operating systems.
Domain Controller	In each Site that will contain an Exchange server there must be at least one writable Domain Controller running one of the above operating systems.
Functional Level	Windows Server 2003 Functional mode or higher.

EXCHANGE ORGANIZATION PRE-REQUISITES

The existing Exchange Organization in this guide is Exchange Server 2007, and all Exchange servers must be at least Exchange Server 2007 with Service Pack 2. There are no other specific requirements however you should run the Exchange Pre-Deployment Analyzer to look for health or configuration issues that might prevent a successful migration.

RUNNING THE EXCHANGE PRE-DEPLOYMENT ANALYZER

The Exchange Pre-Deployment Analyzer performs a readiness scan of your existing environment and reports on configuration items that are either critical (i.e. will prevent Exchange Server 2010 deployment) or warning (i.e. will not prevent deployment but may cause issues in some scenarios)

You can download the Exchange Pre-Deployment Analyzer from Microsoft and run it from any server that meets these system requirements:

- Installed operating system is either: o Windows 7
- Windows Server 2008 R2
- Windows Server 2008 with SP2
- Windows Vista with SP2
- Windows Server 2003 with SP2
- Dot.NET Framework 2.0 or later

Installation of the Exchange Pre-Deployment Analyzer is very simple. Apart from the license agreement there is nothing to configure and you can accept the default install options.

After the install is complete there is an option to launch the Exchange Pre-Deployment Analyzer immediately, or you can launch it later from the Start Menu under **All Programs > Exchange Readiness Tools.**

1. When you first launch the Exchange Pre-Deployment Analyzer it will ask you whether you want to check for updates, and whether you want to join the Customer Experience Improvement Program.

2. I recommend always checking for the latest updates before running the Exchange Pre-Deployment Analyzer, but the Customer Experience Improvement Program opt-in is up to you.

3. After updating the Exchange Pre-Deployment Analyzer you can run a readiness scan of the environment. Click on **Select options for a new scan.**

4. The Exchange Pre-Deployment Analyzer will select a Global Catalog server automatically to use for the scan. You can also manually specify the Domain Controller that you wish to connect to. The scan will run using the currently logged on user credentials so you also have the option to specify different credentials if your current logon does not have the necessary rights to the Active Directory.

5. If you're happy with the selected Domain Controller and credentials click on **Connect to the Active Directory server.**

6. You can enter an identifying label for the scan to make it a little easier to locate the report later on, however it is optional.

7. The default scope for the readiness can is the entire Exchange organization. In more complex environments you might wish to limit the scope of the scan to particular servers or an administrative group, but in this example I will scan the entire organization.

8. When the scan is complete click on **View a report of this Best Practices scan.**

9. The Exchange Pre-Deployment Analyzer report will open and display the **Critical Issues**. These are the issues that will prevent an Exchange Server 2010 deployment from commencing and must be resolved before you can proceed with your deployment project. Click on any of the reported issues to see more details about that item.

10. The **All Issues** tab of the report will display both critical and warning items. Warning items are those issues that will not prevent an Exchange Server 2010 deployment but that may cause problems under some circumstances.

11. Each warning item must be investigated to determine whether it applies to your situation or not. If you are uncertain then take caution and resolve the warning items before you begin the deployment project.

12. The **Informational Items** tab of the report presents some useful information for planning your deployment of Exchange Server 2010, such as the Active Directory domains in the Forest and the number of Exchange mailboxes in the organization.

This Brings Us To The First Check Post In This Migration Project – The Planners Check Post!

One should have completed all the below by now and have tick marks against each of the titles. Only then should a migrator proceed ahead at this stage. Page references to the topics earlier above have been provided for quick reference of the engineer.

- Downloaded the Exchange Server 2010 software and tools.
- Run the Exchange Profile Analyzer.
- Identified mailbox storage quotas.
- Identified room and equipment mailboxes and public folders.
- Audited the network for PST file usage.
- Identified public folder usage.
- Identified the email routing topology, and the configuration processes for all involved systems.
- Identified all Outlook and other mail clients on the network.
- Identified mail-integrated applications and devices.
- Plan your SSL certificates.
- Plan your IP addresses.
- Run the Exchange Pre-Deployment Analyzer and resolved all issues.

PREPARING TO INSTALL EXCHANGE SERVER 2010

There are six new Exchange Server 2010 servers being deployed as part of this guide. These will be:

Head Office
HE2K10-CH1 - Client Access/Hub Transport
HE2K10-CH2 - Client Access/Hub Transport
HE2K10-MB1 - Mailbox
HE2K10-MB2 - Mailbox

Remote Office
R2K10-CAHT - Client Access/Hub Transport
R2K10-MB - Mailbox

Let's first begin with looking at the different sizing options we have for these exchange servers. Microsoft has profound detailed explanative documents on this. Especially as getting the hardware specifications correct for Exchange Server 2010 servers can be a complex task depending on the size of your environment, various parts of the solutions are needed to be taken into account, like the number of mailbox users, the roles that will be installed on each server, and the amount of email data in your organization.

It's hence best to refer to the following Microsoft documents.

http://technet.microsoft.com/en-us/library/dd346699.aspx - Process Config and Exchange Performance

http://technet.microsoft.com/en-us/library/dd346700.aspx - Memory Config

http://technet.microsoft.com/en-us/library/dd346701.aspx - Server Role Ratios

http://technet.microsoft.com/en-us/library/dd298121.aspx - Capacity planning and multiple role

http://technet.microsoft.com/en-us/library/ee832795.aspx - CA and HT combination.

http://msexchangeteam.com/archive/2009/11/09/453117.aspx - Mailbox Role Capacity Calculator

Up to 50% increase in mailboxes after migration to E2K10. – Check for this!! !

http://msexchangeteam.com/archive/2011/01/04/457429.aspx - Infrastructure planning and design.

PREPARING THE EXCHANGE SERVERS

OPERATING SYSTEM VERSIONS

Install the new server with one of the following operating systems:

• Windows Server 2008 Standard/Enterprise x64 with Service Pack 2

• Windows Server 2008 R2 Standard/Enterprise x64, preferably with Service Pack 1

Enterprise Edition of Windows Server is only required for Mailbox servers that will be members of a Database Availability Group.

BASIC CONFIGURATIONS

Apply the following basic configuration items to each server.

• Computer name (you can't rename the server after Exchange Server 2010 is installed)

• Static IP address configuration

• Join to the Active Directory domain as a member server

• Time zone

• Automatic updates settings

• Enable Remote Desktop

• Activate Windows

EXCHANGE SERVER 2010 PRE-REQUISITES

The process to install these is different depending on the server operating system you have installed. In this guide Windows Server 2008 R2 SP1 is being used for the new Exchange servers, so the pre-requisites installation for that version of Windows will be demonstrated.

If you need to use Windows Server 2008 (not R2) in your environment refer to Microsoft TechNet for the latest guidance on installing the pre-requisites.

Exchange Server 2010 setup includes an option to automatically install the required Windows features for the Exchange Server roles being installed, however some of these pre-requisites are needed for setup itself, so it is easier to install them in advance.

Detailed information about this is found in the Microsoft KB article no **bb691354**.aspx

PREPARING CLIENT ACCESS/HUB TRANSPORT SERVERS

In this guide we'll be deploying the Head Office Client Access/Hub Transport servers in a load-balanced Client Access Server Array (CAS Array). This involves setting up a Windows Network Load Balancing (NLB) cluster. For that to occur each of the Head Office Client Access/Hub Transport servers are configured with a second network interface.

You can skip ahead to the next section if you're not planning to deploy a load-balanced CAS Array in any of your sites.

CONFIGURING THE SECOND NETWORK INTERFACE FOR NLB

The second network interfaces as used to form the NLB cluster and perform load balancing of connections received on the NLB Virtual IP.

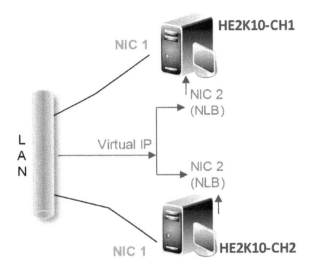

The NLB network interfaces need the following configurations:
- Static IP addresses
- No default gateway
- No DNS registration

1. To make the two interfaces easier to identify later it is useful to rename them according to their purpose.
2. **Right-click** the NLB interface and choose **Properties**. Then select **Internet Protocol Version 4** and click on **Properties.**
3. Configure the static IP address and subnet mask, but leave the default gateway and DNS servers blank, then click **Advanced**
4. Select the **DNS** tab and then clear the tick box to **Register this connection's addresses in DNS.**
5. Click **OK**, **OK** and then **Close** to apply the configuration.

INSTALLING THE MICROSOFT OFFICE FILTER PACK

Servers that will host the Hub Transport server role require the Microsoft Filter Pack which we downloaded at the start of this guide (page 6) so that Exchange can index text content within files that are in the Office formats.

By installing the Filter Pack before you install Exchange Server 2010, Exchange setup will automatically register the filters with the Exchange Search service.

Run the setup file to install the Microsoft Filter Pack.

There are no installation options to choose, simply accept the license agreement and let the Filter Pack install itself.

INSTALLING OPERATING SYSTEM ROLES AND FEATURES

After installing the Filter Pack run the following commands from an elevated Windows PowerShell console. First import the ServerManager PowerShell module.

```
PS C:\> Import-Module ServerManager
```

Next install the roles and features that are required for Exchange Server 2010 Client Access and Hub Transport roles.

Note that this is a single-line command and will automatically restart the server as well. If you don't want to automatically restart the server just remove the **–restart** switch from the end of the command line.

For Client Access servers that will be members of a Client Access Server Array use this command.

```
PS C:\> Add-WindowsFeature NET-Framework,RSAT-ADDS,Web-Server,Web-Basic-Auth,Web-
Windows-Auth,Web-Metabase,Web-Net-Ext,Web-Lgcy-Mgmt-Console,WAS-Process-Model,RSAT-Web-
Server,Web-ISAPI-Ext,Web-Digest-Auth,Web-Dyn-Compression,NET-HTTP-Activation,RPC-Over-
HTTP-Proxy, NLB -Restart
```

For standalone Client Access servers use this command.

```
PS C:\> Add-WindowsFeature NET-Framework,RSAT-ADDS,Web-Server,Web-Basic-Auth,Web-Windows-
Auth,Web-Metabase,Web-Net-Ext,Web-Lgcy-Mgmt-Console,WAS-Process-Model,RSAT-Web-Server,Web-
ISAPI-Ext,Web-Digest-Auth,Web-Dyn-Compression,NET-HTTP-Activation,RPC-Over-HTTP-Proxy, -
Restart
```

After the restart launch another elevated Windows PowerShell console and run the following command which is required for Client Access servers.

```
PS C:\> Set-Service NetTcpPortSharing -StartupType Automatic
```

PREPARING MAILBOX SERVERS

CONFIGURING THE SECOND NETWORK INTERFACE FOR DATABASE REPLICATION

The second network interfaces on Database Availability Group members are used to separate database replication traffic from client traffic. Although it is not mandatory to have a dedicated replication network it is recommended as a best practice.

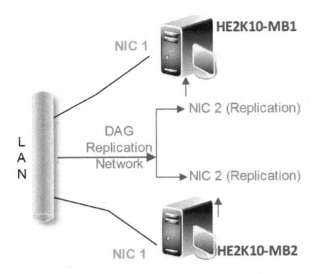

If you are not deploying any Database Availability Groups then you can skip this section.
The NLB network interfaces need the following configurations:
• Static IP addresses
• No default gateway
• No DNS registration

1. To make the two interfaces easier to identify later it is useful to rename them according to their purpose.
2. Right-click the Replication interface and choose **Properties**. Then select **Internet Protocol Version 4** and click on **Properties.**
3. Configure the static IP address and subnet mask, and leave the default gateway and DNS servers blank, and then click **Advanced.**
4. Select the **DNS** tab and then clear the tick box to **Register this connection's addresses in DNS.**
5. **Clicks OK, OK** and then **Close** to apply the configuration.

INSTALLING THE MICROSOFT OFFICE FILTER PACK

As with Hub Transport servers, the servers that will host the Mailbox server role require the Microsoft Filter Pack which we downloaded at the start of this guide so that Exchange can index text content within files that are in the Office formats.

By installing the Filter Pack before you install Exchange Server 2010, Exchange setup will automatically register the filters with the Exchange Search service.

Run the setup file to install the Microsoft Filter Pack.

There are no installation options to choose, simply accept the license agreement and let the Filter Pack install itself.

INSTALLING OPERATING SYSTEM ROLES AND FEATURES

After installing the Filter Pack run the following commands from an elevated Windows PowerShell console. First import the Server Manager PowerShell module.

```
PS C:\> Import-Module ServerManager
```

Next install the roles and features that are required for Exchange Server 2010 Mailbox server role.

Note that this command line will automatically restart the server as well. If you don't want to automatically restart the server just remove the **–restart** switch from the end of the command line.

For the Mailbox servers that will be deployed in a Database Availability Group use this command line that includes the Failover Clustering feature.

```
PS C:\> Add-WindowsFeature NET-Framework,RSAT-ADDS,Web-Server,Web-Basic-Auth,Web-Windows-
Auth,Web-Metabase,Web-Net-Ext,Web-Lgcy-Mgmt-Console,WAS-Process-Model,RSAT-Web-Server,
Failover-Clustering –Restart
```

For the Mailbox server that will not be a member of a Database Availability Group use this command:

```
PS C:\> Add-WindowsFeature NET-Framework,RSAT-ADDS,Web-Server,Web-Basic-Auth,Web-Windows-
Auth,Web-Metabase,Web-Net-Ext,Web-Lgcy-Mgmt-Console,WAS-Process-Model,RSAT-Web-Server –
Restart
```

CONFIGURING ADDITIONAL STORAGE

The Mailbox servers need to be configured with some additional disk storage for the Exchange databases and transaction logs.

It is important to give Exchange Server 2010 Mailbox servers disk storage that will perform well for the workload of the server. Every Exchange environment is different and needs the correct storage configuration.

No matter the size of your environment I always recommend that you use the Exchange 2010 Mailbox Server Role Requirements Calculator of this guide to calculate your storage requirements.

In this guide each of the Mailbox servers is configured with a 20 GB volume for the transaction logs, and a 40 GB volume for the database files, which is sufficient for the sizes of the mailboxes in this example environment.

In the case of the Head Office Mailbox servers the log and database volumes are mounted with the same drive letters on each server (i.e. logs on E:\ drive and databases on F:\ drive).

This is because a Database Availability Group requires matching storage paths on any servers that will be holding replicas of the same databases. If a database is stored in F:\Database then that same path must be available on the other servers that will replicate that database.

PREPARING ACTIVE DIRECTORY

BACKING UP ACTIVE DIRECTORY

The Active Directory Schema update for Exchange Server 2010 is a fairly low risk exercise; however the impact can be very big on the rare chance that something does go wrong with it.

So before you proceed with the schema update you need to make sure that you have a current, working backup of your Active Directory, and are familiar with the process for restoring Active Directory.

If you've never performed these operations before then you may wish to practice in a lab environment before you update your production Active Directory for Exchange Server 2010.

You could either search for the following KB Articles **cc778772** (2003 Server) and **cc816916** (2008 Server) on Google or Microsoft sites to get the full steps.

APPLYING THE EXCHANGE SERVER 2010 SCHEMA UPDATE

You must perform these steps with an account that is a member of the Enterprise Admins and Schema Admins groups.

The server that you run the schema update on must reside in the same Active Directory Site as the Schema Master. You can just use one of your new servers that you have prepared for Exchange Server 2010.

If you have not already done so, download the Exchange Server 2010 files from Microsoft and extract them to a folder on the server.

Launch a Command Prompt, navigate to the directory that has the setup files located in it, and run the Exchange Server 2010 schema update.

```
C:\Admin\ex2010> setup /preparead
```

Wait for the schema update to complete successfully.

```
Welcome to Microsoft Exchange Server 2010 Unattended Setup
Preparing Exchange Setup
Copying Setup Files                                      COMPLETED
No server roles will be installed
Performing Microsoft Exchange Server Prerequisite Check
Organization Checks COMPLETED
Setup is going to prepare the organization for Exchange 2010 by using 'Setup /P
repareAD'. No Exchange 2007 server roles have been detected in this topology. Af
ter this operation, you will not be able to install any Exchange 2003 or Exchang
e 2007 servers.
Configuring Microsoft Exchange Server
Organization Preparation                                COMPLETED
The Microsoft Exchange Server setup operation completed successfully.
```

If you have an Active Directory with multiple Domain Controllers you should wait for the new schema to replicate throughout the network before proceeding to the next steps.

* * * INSTALLING EXCHANGE SERVER 2010 * * *

UNDERSTANDING THE ORDER OF INSTALLATION

The Exchange Server 2010 server roles need to be installed in a particular order during a migration. This is to ensure that all of the correct functionality is in place to support Exchange Server 2007 and Exchange Server 2010 mailboxes, message routing, and other features during the migration.

The order of deployment is: *Edge Transport and Unified Messaging servers are not covered by this guide*

1. Client Access

2. Hub Transport

3. Mailbox

The Exchange Server 2010 deployment also needs to begin at the internet-facing site of the organization, so that external access can function correctly during the migration period.

UNDERSTANDING EXCHANGE SERVER ADMINISTRATION DURING TRANSITION

After you've installed your first Exchange Server 2010 server into the organization you need to be aware of a few "rules" for administering Exchange.

- Manage Exchange server settings using the matching version of the management tools. For example, configure Exchange 2010 server settings only with the Exchange 2010 console or shell.
- Transport and Journal rules (if you are using them) are copied from the Exchange 2007 configuration container to a new container for Exchange 2010. This means that at the time you install Exchange 2010 the rules will be copied as-is and will match. However any changes you make to either the 2007 or 2010 version of the rules will not automatically synchronize with the other version.
- Manage mailboxes using the matching version of the management tools. For example, configure mailbox settings for an Exchange 2010 mailbox user only with the Exchange 2010 console or shell.
- Although you can view some settings for servers or mailboxes using the non-matching version of the management tools, you should not try to modify any of them with the non-matching version

A WARNING ABOUT AUTODISCOVER

Autodiscover is a service that allows compatible Outlook versions and mobile devices to automatically detect and configure a user's mailbox settings. When the Client Access server role is installed into an Exchange organization it automatically registers the Autodiscover service in Active Directory for the Site that the server is located in.

Outlook clients will connect to Autodiscover using HTTPS (SSL), but the new Exchange Server 2010 Client Access server is configured with a self-signed SSL certificate when it is first installed. This can lead to certificate warnings for your end users who are running Outlook 2007 or Outlook 2010.

To avoid these certificate warnings you may wish to install the first server outside of business hours, so that you have time to resolve the certificate warnings without impacting your end users.

There are three ways to quickly resolve the SSL certificate warnings:
- Add the Exchange server certificate to the Trusted Root Certification Authorities on all of your end user computers using a Group Policy (not recommended)
- Issuing a new SSL certificate from a trusted, private Certificate Authority on your network (not ideal, but resolves the issue for computers that are domain members)
- Purchasing a new SSL certificate from a commercial Certificate Authority and installing it on the Exchange server (this is the best solution, but will of course require you to spend money)
- In an upcoming section of this guide we'll go through the process of generating a new SSL certificate request and installing the certificate on the Exchange server.

INSTALLING THE HEAD OFFICE CLIENT ACCESS/HUB TRANSPORT SERVERS

The first server to install is the Head Office Client Access and Hub Transport servers. In this guide the server roles are being deployed together on two servers, HE-2K10-CH1 and HE-2K10-CH2.

INSTALLING EXCHANGE SERVER 2010 IN GRAPHICAL MODE

From the location that you extracted the Exchange Server 2010 setup files launch the Setup.exe file. At the setup splash screen, if any of the setup pre-requisites (i.e. .NET Framework 3.5 SP1 and Windows PowerShell v2) are missing you can click on the links to download and install those items then and there.

While you will get many articles from various blogs and Microsoft itself as to how one should install Exchange using the Graphical Mode, you should take care to follow what each splash screen says and it's pretty straight forward and I recommend for all first times to use the graphical mode to instill confidence in them.

I will hence concentrate on how to install Microsoft Exchange 2010 using command prompt for more senior administrators.

INSTALLING EXCHANGE SERVER 2010 IN COMMAND-LINE MODE

In this guide we're installing two Client Access/Hub Transport servers in the Head Office location.

FIRST SERVER

The first server is a typical install and you can install it using the graphical installation interface of Exchange or use the more tasking command prompt. As command prompt is a little trickier due to command syntax, order, appropriate options, I have explained this in more detail. One can use this method to install the First Server too, however if you wish to use the normal graphical installation you are welcome to do so.

SECOND SERVER

To install an Exchange Server 2010 server from the command-line there are two basic setup parameters to understand:
- **/mode:install** – sets the setup mode to "install" for a new server
- **/roles:c,h,t** – installs the Client Access, Hub Transport, and Management Tools roles
- **/InstallWindowsComponents** – installs any pre-requisites that may have been missed during the preparation of the server

Because this is a Client Access server we'll also be using the **/ExternalCASServerDomain** parameter to pre-configure the virtual directories with the correct public name.

From a command-line navigate to the folder where the extracted setup files are located and run the following command.

C:\Admin\ex2010>setup /mode:install /roles:c,h,t /ExternalCASServerDomain:mai l.exchangeserverpro.net /InstallWindowsComponents

Setup will start and run in unattended mode.

```
C:\Admin\ex2010>setup /mode:install /roles:c,h,t /ExternalCASServerDomain:mai
l.exchangeserverpro.net
Welcome to Microsoft Exchange Server 2010 Unattended Setup
Setup will continue momentarily, unless you press any key and cancel the
installation. By continuing the installation process, you agree to the license
terms of Microsoft Exchange Server 2010.
If you don't accept these license terms, please cancel the installation. To
review the license terms, please go to
http://go.microsoft.com/fwlink/?LinkId=150127&clcid=0x409/
Press any key to cancel setup................
No key presses were detected. Setup will continue.
Preparing Exchange Setup
Copying Setup Files COMPLETED
The following server role(s) will be installed
Languages
Management Tools
Hub Transport Role
Client Access Role
Performing Microsoft Exchange Server Prerequisite Check
```

```
Configuring Prerequisites COMPLETED
Language Pack Checks COMPLETED
Hub Transport Role Checks COMPLETED
Client Access Role Checks COMPLETED
Configuring Microsoft Exchange Server
Preparing Setup COMPLETED
Stopping Services COMPLETED
Copying Exchange Files COMPLETED
Language Files COMPLETED
Restoring Services COMPLETED
Languages COMPLETED
Exchange Management Tools COMPLETED
Hub Transport Server Role COMPLETED
Client Access Server Role COMPLETED
Finalizing Setup COMPLETED
The Microsoft Exchange Server setup operation completed successfully.
Setup has made changes to operating system settings that require a reboot to
take effect. Please reboot this server prior to placing it into production.
```

Restart the server when setup has completed, and then run Windows Update to ensure that the latest updates are installed before proceeding further.

FIRST LOOK AT THE EXCHANGE SERVER 2010 MANAGEMENT TOOLS

Since this might be your first experience with Exchange Server 2010 let's take a moment to quickly look at the new management tools that you'll be using as you follow the rest of this guide.

You'll find the new management tools in the Start Menu under **All Programs > Microsoft Exchange Server 2010**. Feel free to pin them to the top of the Start Menu for easy access.

EXCHANGE MANAGEMENT CONSOLE

The Exchange Management Console (or EMC) is the graphical administrative interface for Exchange Server 2010. Note that if you see a warning about the Exchange product key when you launch the EMC it can be ignored for now as we will see how to configure that a little later in this guide. It is the EMC where you will be performing many of the administration tasks that one would normally perform in Active Directory Users & Computers, as well as configuring the Exchange organization and servers. Not that you cannot still do it in ADUC but its Microsoft's way of providing an Exchange in-house all in one access.

EXCHANGE MANAGEMENT SHELL

The Exchange Management Shell (or EMS) is a PowerShell-based command-line environment for managing Exchange Server 2010. Everything that can be done using the EMC can also be done using the EMS; however the EMS is comparatively more powerful and has some administrative capabilities that the EMC does not as it uses PowerShell – Microsoft's advance command prompt utility and hence is an advance administrator's useful tool.

DEPLOYING THE SSL CERTIFICATE

Now that the new Exchange Server 2010 Client Access server has been installed you may encounter certificate warnings for Outlook 2007 and Outlook 2010 users.

As mentioned on page 24 you can resolve these errors in one of three ways:

- Add the Exchange Server certificate to the Trusted Root Certification Authorities on all of your end user computers using a Group Policy (not recommended).
- Issuing a new SSL certificate from a trusted, private Certificate Authority on your network (not ideal, but resolves the issue for computers that are domain members)
- Purchasing a new SSL certificate from a commercial Certificate Authority and installing it on the Exchange Server (this is the best solution, but will of course require you to spend money)

Even though you might already have an SSL certificate installed on your Exchange Server 2007 servers you will need a new certificate that matches the names of the new Exchange 2010 servers.
Some environments may also have avoided using a SAN certificate for their Exchange Server 2007 deployment, which was possible by making some configuration changes. I don't recommend trying to take the same shortcuts with Exchange 2010.

If you're not already familiar with SAN certificates, they are simply an SSL certificate with multiple names configure for it, instead of just a single name. This allows the one SAN certificate to be used for multiple services on Exchange Server 2010 that may answer to different names, for example:

- Some SSL connections will be made to the server's FQDN
- Some SSL connections will be made to a DNS alias (mail.chetanpawar.com)

For the scope of this guide we will generate a certificate request for a new SAN certificate, submitting it to a Certificate Authority, and then installing the issued certificate on the new Exchange Server 2010 Client Access server. Let's start by generating the certificate to begin with.

1.   **GENERATING A NEW CERTIFICATE REQUEST**

a) In the **Exchange Management Console** navigate to **Server Configuration**. Right-click the server and choose **New Exchange Certificate.**

b) **Enter a friendly name for the new certificate. In this example I have named it "Exchange 2010 Certificate". Click Next to continue.**

c) Although wildcard certificates are supported in Exchange Server 2010 it is recommended to use a SAN (Subject Alternative Name) certificate instead. **Do not enable wildcard certificate** at this stage. Click **Next** to continue.

d) Next we can configure the names for each of the Exchange services that are secured with the SSL certificate. Refer back to the names that you discovered during the planning stage of this guide.

e) We're not configuring Sharing for this organization, so the first up is the Outlook Web App service.

f) Expand the Outlook Web App section and tick the boxes for Intranet and Internet access. You'll notice that the names are automatically filled in using the server's FQDN and the external name that was provided during setup. If you didn't specify a public name during setup you will need to enter the names manually here instead.

g) Remove the Exchange Server 2007 server names from the internal OWA names. You can also add in any additional Client Access servers that you plan to deploy in your organization, separating the names with commas, unless you plan to create separate certificates for each of them in which case only enter the server names you need on this certificate.

h) We must note that some certificate authorities have different licensing models that may not permit the use of one certificate across multiple servers, or may charge for additional licenses.

i) Next configure the ActiveSync domain name. For ease of administration and configuration I am using the same name as for Outlook Web App.

j) Next are the Web Services, Outlook Anywhere and Autodiscover names. Once again I am using the same name of "mail.chetanpawar.com".

k) For Autodiscover the additional name of "autodiscover.chetanpawar.com" is configured. If you have more than one SMTP namespace for your organization you should add Autodiscover names for those domains as well.

l) POP and IMAP tend to be less common these days and aren't included in this guide, nor is Unified Messaging.

m) The Hub Transport server also requires SSL for secure SMTP communications over the internet. In this example I am using the name "mail.chetanpawar.com" again.

n) A legacy name is required if you are planning to gradually transition services and data from Exchange 2007 to Exchange 2010, as I am doing in this guide.

o) Configure legacy names for each of the namespaces in the organization, in this example "legacy.chetanpawar.com".

p) When all of the services have been configured click **Next** to proceed to the next step of the New Exchange Certificate wizard.

q) Confirm that all of the required names have been included in the certificate. You can add any additional names at this stage before clicking **Next** to continue.

r) Next configure the organization and location information for the certificate, and choose a location to generate the certificate request file.

Most commercial Certificate Authorities require that the organization information in the certificate request matches the WHOIS information for the domain name. Refer to the details you collected from the existing SSL certificate. You can also use tools such as http://whois.domaintools.com to check your domain names for the correct information.

s) When you have finished filling out the wizard, click the **New** button to generate the certificate request file.

t) Confirm that the certificate request file was successfully generated.

You will notice that the wizard makes a recommendation as to the type of certificate that is required for your Exchange organization. In most cases a "Unified Communications certificate" will be necessary, which is basically another name for a SAN certificate.

Step 1: Based on the information you provided, you must use a Unified Communications certificate. Please get the certificate from a certification authority.

Step 2: Use the Complete Pending Request wizard to map the certificate to the certificate request created on the server.

Step 3: Assign the Exchange services to the certificate using the Assign Services to Certificate wizard.

The wizard will show a very valuable suggestion about this Unified Communications certificate. I have managed to screen shot one for reference here.

Although you can generate the certificate from a private Certificate Authority it is recommended to use a public Certificate Authority such as Digicert20. There are other providers that are also fine to use but I personally tend to use http://www.digicert.com/unified-communications-ssl-tls.htm because the price and unlimited server license are good value, and they allow unlimited reissues if you make a mistake with the names you configured in the certificate request.

Whichever Certificate Authority you choose for your SSL certificate, simply follow their instructions for submitting your certificate request and receiving the generated certificate from them.

2.   INSTALLING THE NEW CERTIFICATE

After you have acquired the certificate from the Certificate Authority return to the Exchange Management Console, navigate to Server Configuration and select the same Exchange server that made the certificate request.

a) In the lower pane right-click the certificate and choose **Complete Pending Request.**

b) At the Complete Pending Request wizard click the **Browse** button.

c) Browse to the location of the certificate file that you downloaded from the Certificate Authority and open it.

d) Click on the **Complete** button to complete the pending request.

e) Confirm that the new certificate was imported successfully and click **Finish.**

f) The new certificate now appears in the list of valid certificates for the server.

In some networks the firewall may prevent the Exchange server from connecting to the Microsoft Certificate Revocation List (CRL) to verify the newly installed certificate. This will prevent you from enabling the certificate for any services.

To resolve the issue you may need to modify your firewall configuration to allow the Exchange server to connect outbound on TCP port 443, or configure the server to use a proxy server on your network to make the outbound connection.

3.   ASSIGN THE NEW CERTIFICATE TO EXCHANGE SERVER 2010

a) With the valid certificate installed it is now time to assign it to the Exchange Server 2010 services. Right-click the new certificate and choose **Assign Services to Certificate.**

b) Add the new Exchange server to the list if it is not already there, and click Next to continue.

c) Choose the services to assign to the certificate. In this example the certificate was created for IIS and SMTP services. Click Next to continue.

d) Complete the wizard to assign the services to the new certificate. You will be prompted to overwrite the existing self-signed certificate, so choose **Yes** to that prompt.

e) That completes the configuration of the SSL certificate for the internet-facing Client Access server.

4.   EXPORTING AND IMPORTING THE SSL CERTIFICATE

As we are doing a two internet-facing Client Access servers deployment for high availability, we will use the same SSL certificate that is being used on the first server for the second one too. We will hence need to export it from the first Client Access server and import it into the second server.

a) In the **Exchange Management Console** navigate to **Server Configuration** and select the **first** Client Access server. Right-click the **Exchange 2010 Certificate** that was installed earlier and choose Export Exchange Certificate.

b) Click the **Browse** button and choose a location and file name to save the exported certificate. Enter a password to protect the exported certificate, and then click **Export**.

c) When the export operation has completed click the **Finish** button.

d) Next, right-click on the second Client Access server and choose **Import Exchange Certificate**.

e) Click the **Browse** button and then locate and select the exported certificate. Enter the same password that you used when exporting the certificate, and then click **Next**.

f) If you have installed more Client Access servers in your organization you can add them to the import operation as well. When you've added all of your servers click **Next** to continue.
g) Now click **Import** when you are ready to begin the operation.
h) When the import operation is complete click the **Finish** button.
i) Finally, repeat the same steps you performed on *(assign the new certificate to exchange server 2010)* to assign the certificate to Exchange services.

INSTALLING THE CLIENT ACCESS SERVER ARRAY

It is recommended to configure CAS Arrays in each site that will contain Mailbox servers before you deploy any Mailbox servers in that site, even if you do not plan to use load-balanced CAS Arrays for high availability.

The reason for this is that each Mailbox database has an attribute called **RPCClientAccessServer**. This attribute is set automatically to the CAS Array name if one has already been set up in that AD site. Otherwise it is set to the name of one of the Client Access servers in that AD site.

If you then install a CAS Array later on the **RPCClientAccessServer** attribute on the databases does not automatically update to the name of the new CAS Array. Though you can manually update it, the client Outlook profiles do not always pick up that change automatically, which complicates the process of moving to a high availability configuration later on, or replacing the Client Access server if the need arises.

1. CREATING THE NLB CLUSTER – (*Optional Configuration*)

This is an optional section and can be skipped where Windows Network Load Balancing is NOT being used for the CAS Array. Hence, if you are not planning to use NLB for high availability, please move on to the next section – **Creating a DNS Record**.

Logon to the first Client Access server and launch the Network Load Balancing Manager from Administrative tools.

a) From the **Cluster** menu choose **New**.
b) Enter the name of the first Client Access server, and then click **Connect**.
c) Choose the interface that is to be used for the cluster, and then click **Next**.
d) Accept the default host parameters and click **Next**.
e) Click **Add** and enter the IPv4 address for the NLB cluster, then click **OK**.
f) Click **Next** to continue.
g) Enter a name for the NLB cluster. In this guide we'll use outlook.chetanpawar.com as this is the only NLB cluster being deployed. If you are planning to deploy NLB clusters in multiple sites you can consider using a different naming convention that incorporates an identifier for each site. The NLB cluster name can be independent of the CAS Array name if you wish.
h) Highlight the default port rules and click **Remove**.
i) Click the **Add** button and add a port rule for TCP port 80 with Single affinity.

j) Repeat the same steps to add port rules for:
- TCP port 135
- TCP port 443
- TCP port 1024-65535

k) Click **Finish** to complete the creation of the NLB cluster.
l) At this stage you should have a single host NLB cluster that is successfully converged.
m) Right-click the cluster name and choose **Add Host to Cluster**.
n) Enter the name of the second Client Access server and click **Connect.**
o) Choose the interface to be used for the cluster and click **Next**.
p) Accept the default Host Parameters and click **Next.**
q) There are no changes necessary for the port rules, so click **Finish.**
r) You should now have a dual host NLB cluster that is successfully converged.

2.   CREATING A DNS RECORD

The CAS Array needs a DNS record. In your internal DNS zone create a new host record for the CAS Array name and IP address. In this example I'm using **outlook.chetanpawar.com** for the CAS Array in the Head Office location.

The DNS record should point to the virtual IP of the NLB cluster, or hardware load balancer if you have gone down that road instead. If you have not deployed a load-balancer of any kind then point the DNS record for the CAS Array at the IP address of your Client Access server in the site.
If DNS is configured correctly you should be able to successfully ping the DNS name of the CAS Array.

3.   CREATING THE CLIENT ACCESS ARRAY

Launch the Exchange Management Shell on one of the Exchange 2010 servers and run the following command.

```
[PS] C:\>New-ClientAccessArray -Name HeadOffice -Site HeadOffice -Fqdn
outlook.chetanpawar.com
Creating a new session for implicit remoting of "New-ClientAccessArray"
command...
Name Site Fqdn Members
---- ---- ---- -------
HeadOffice HeadOffice outlook.chetanpawar.com {HE-2K10-CH1, HE-2K10-CH2}
```

The CAS Array configuration is complete.

INSTALLING THE HEAD OFFICE MAILBOX SERVERS

The next servers that we are going to install are the Head Office Mailbox servers.

When you install a new Mailbox server Exchange setup creates a mailbox database for that server. There are a few things worth noting about this:

- All mailbox databases on Exchange Server 2010 Mailbox servers must have a name that is unique throughout the entire organization (not just that server)
- The mailbox database is created by default in the same file system path that Exchange is installed into
- Exchange Server 2010 no longer uses storage groups. The transaction logs are just considered part of the database
- It is still best practice to separate your transaction logs and database files onto different volumes

We're going to use the command-line to run Exchange setup again, this time with a different set of parameters:-

- **/mode:install** – sets the setup mode to "install" for a new server
- **/roles:m,t** – installs the Mailbox, and Management Tools roles
- **/InstallWindowsComponents** – installs any pre-requisites that may have been missed during the preparation of the server
- **/MdbName** – the name of the mailbox database created by setup
- **/DbFilePath** – the path for the database file created by setup
- **/LogFolderPath** – the path to the transaction logs folder for the database created by setup.

From a command-line navigate to the folder where the extracted setup files are located and run the following command.....

```
C:\Admin\ex2010>setup /mode:install /roles:m,t /installwindowscomponents /mdb
name:MB-HE-01 /dbfilepath:F:\Data\MB-HE-01\MB-HE-01.edb /logfolderpath:E:\Logs\M
B-HE-01
```

Running this command will start the unattended setup as well as if all settings and earlier configurations are correct will give an output as below:

```
Welcome to Microsoft Exchange Server 2010 Unattended Setup
Setup will continue momentarily, unless you press any key and cancel the
installation. By continuing the installation process, you agree to the license
terms of Microsoft Exchange Server 2010.
If you don't accept these license terms, please cancel the installation. To
review the license terms, please go to
http://go.microsoft.com/fwlink/?LinkId=150127&clcid=0x409/
Press any key to cancel setup................
No key presses were detected. Setup will continue.
Preparing Exchange Setup
Copying Setup Files COMPLETED
The following server role(s) will be installed
Languages
```

```
Management Tools
Mailbox Role
Performing Microsoft Exchange Server Prerequisite Check
Configuring Prerequisites                              COMPLETED
Language Pack Checks                                   COMPLETED
Mailbox Role Checks                                    COMPLETED
Configuring Microsoft Exchange Server
Preparing Setup                                        COMPLETED
Stopping Services                                      COMPLETED
Copying Exchange Files                                 COMPLETED
Language Files                                         COMPLETED
Restoring Services                                     COMPLETED
Languages                                              COMPLETED
Exchange Management Tools                              COMPLETED
Mailbox Server Role                                    COMPLETED
Finalizing Setup                                       COMPLETED
The Microsoft Exchange Server setup operation completed successfully.
Setup has made changes to operating system settings that require a reboot to
take effect. Please reboot this server prior to placing it into production.
```

You can use the same command-line to install the other Head Office Mailbox server (if you are deploying more than one), just make sure that you change the database name, database file path, and log folder path to be unique.

Restart the head office Mailbox servers when unattended setup has completed, and then run Windows Update to ensure they have the latest updates.

There are no other configuration tasks to perform on these servers at this stage, so you can proceed with the installation of other servers next.

INSTALLING THE BRANCH OFFICE CLIENT ACCESS/HUB TRANSPORT SERVER

The next server we'll be installing is the branch office Client Access/Hub Transport server. If you are not deploying any branch office sites in your environment you can skip this section.

Because we are installing a new Client Access server into a site we need to once again consider Autodiscover and the potential impact of the server's self-signed SSL certificate.

As with the head office Client Access server installation I recommend performing the branch office deployment out of business hours so that you have time to provision a new SSL certificate on the server.

This Client Access server is not internet-facing, so we can use a different setup command-line to install it that excludes the /ExternalCASServerDomain parameter. Open a command prompt and run the setup command from the folder where the Exchange installation files have been extracted.

```
C:\Admin\ex2010>setup /mode:install /roles:c,h,t
```

Restart the branch office Client Access/Hub Transport server when unattended setup has completed, and then run Windows Update to ensure it has the latest updates..

INSTALLING THE SSL CERTIFICATE

For the branch office Client Access we're going to provision an SSL certificate using the internal Certificate Authority for the domain. Certificate Services is installed on the head office domain controller and will be used to issue the certificate.

Logon to the branch office Client Access server and open the Exchange Management Console.

1. In the Exchange Management Console navigate to Server Configuration. Right-click the server and choose **New Exchange Certificate**.

2. Enter a **friendly name** for the new certificate. In this example I have named it "Branch Exchange 2010 Certificate". Click **Next** to continue.

3. **Do not enable wildcard certificate** at this stage. Click **Next** to continue.

4. At the **Exchange Configuration** page expand the **Client Access Server (Outlook Web App)** section and check the box for Intranet use. Make sure the **Domain name** has the fully qualified domain name of the server. Click **Next** to continue.

5. If any other names are in the domain list select the server name and click the **Set as common name butto**n, then select and delete the other names. Click **Next** to continue.

6. Fill out the organization information and then choose a path and file name for the certificate request to be stored.

7. Click **Next** to continue, and then **New** to finish creating the certificate request.

8. *Always remember that a Commercial CA can always be used to replace an internal CA.*

9. Open a web browser and navigate to the certificate services web enrollment page on your internal Certificate Authority. Click on **Request a Certificate.**

10. Click on **Advanced Certificate Request**.

11. Click on **Submit a Certificate Request…..**

12. Open the certificate request file in Notepad and copy/paste the contents into the **Saved Request** field, then set the **Certificate Template** to **Web Server**. Click **Submit** to continue.

13. Select **Base 64 Encoded** and then click on **Download Certificate.**

14. Save the file to a location that you can easily locate it for the next steps.

15. Return to the **Exchange Management Console**, navigate to **Server Configuration** and select the branch office server again. Right-click the pending certificate request and choose **Complete Pending Request.**

16. Browse to the location where you saved the new certificate and select it. Click **Complete** to complete the pending certificate request.
17. Click **Finish** when the process has completed.
18. Right-click the new certificate and choose **Assign Services to Certificate.**

19. Make sure the branch office server appears in the list and click **Next** to continue.
20. Tick the box to assign the certificate to **Internet Information Services (IIS)** and then click **Next** to continue.

21. Click **Assign** to complete the process, and then click **Finish.**

INSTALLING THE BRANCH OFFICE MAILBOX SERVER – Again Optional!

The next server we'll be installing is the branch office Mailbox server. *If you are not deploying any branch office sites in your environment you can skip this section.*

As with the head office Mailbox servers we can use the command-line to specify the name and paths for the mailbox database that setup creates. Remember again that the mailbox database name has to be unique within the entire organization, not just on this server.

Log on to the branch office Mailbox server, open a command prompt and run the setup command from the folder where the Exchange installation files have been extracted.

```
C:\Admin\ex2010>setup /mode:install /roles:m,t /installwindowscomponents /mdb
name:MB-BR-01 /dbfilepath:F:\Data\MB-BR-01\MB-BR-01.edb /logfolderpath:E:\Logs\M
B-BR-01
```

Restart the branch office Mailbox server when unattended setup has completed, and then run Windows Update to ensure it has the latest updates.

* * * CONFIGURING EXCHANGE SERVER 2010 * * *

With Exchange Server 2010 installed it is now time to perform some configurations.

THE PRODUCT KEY

By Default the Exchange server will run for 120 days without a product key but one should be entered as soon as possible. Steps to enter the product are as follows:

Launch the **Exchange Management Console** from the Start Menu of one of the servers. A warning will appear listing each Exchange server that is currently unlicensed.

Click **OK** to clear the warning.

In the left pane of the Exchange Management Console navigate to **Server Configuration.**

Right-click the first server in the middle pane and choose **Enter Product key**.

Enter your Product Key in the field and then click the **Enter** button.

For servers with the Mailbox server role installed you will see a message when the Product Key has been applied warning you that the change does not take effect until the Information Store service is restarted. Close the warning dialog box.

For each of the servers with the Mailbox server role installed launch the Exchange Management Shell from the Start Menu and run the following command.

```
[PS] C:\> Restart-Service MSExchangeIS
```

Servers without the Mailbox server role do not need the Information Store service restarted for the new product key to take effect.

CONFIGURING THE CLIENT ACCESS SERVERS

The Client Access servers are responsible for all client connectivity to mailboxes. In this section of the we will see how to configure each of the Client Access services. If there are services that you do not plan to use in your own environment then you can skip those sections.

A.   CONFIGURING OUTLOOK ANYWHERE

✓   In the Exchange Management Console navigate to Server Configuration, Client Access, and select the internet facing Client Access server, in this case HE-2K10-CH1 and HE-2K10-CH2.

✓   Right-click the server and choose Enable Outlook Anywhere.

✓   Enter the external host name that clients will use when connecting to Outlook Anywhere. This is the name that was discovered during the planning phase (page 22) and also a name that you included in the SSL certificate that was installed on the server (page 66).

✓   Next, select the Client authentication method. This should be the same as the authentication method that is configured for Outlook Anywhere on your existing Exchange Server 2007 servers.

✓   Click the Enable button to complete the wizard. A warning is displayed that the new configuration will not take effect for 15 minutes.

Repeat the steps on the other Client Access servers on the network, including those at branch office locations.

B.   CONFIGURING THE OUTLOOK WEB APP VIRTUAL DIRECTORY

- ✓ In the **Exchange Management Console** navigate **to Server Configuration**, **Client Access**, and select the Exchange Server 2010 server that is the internet-facing Client Access server, in this example **HE-2K10-CH1** and **HE-2K10-CH2.**
- ✓ Right-click the OWA virtual directory and choose **Properties**.
- ✓ If you configured an external domain name during Exchange setup then the External URL for Outlook Web App will already be configured.
- ✓ Otherwise, enter the external name that clients will use to connect to Outlook Web App. This is the name that was discovered during the planning phase and also a name that you included in the SSL certificate that was installed on the server.
- ✓ Select the **Authentication** tab. By default Forms-based Authentication is configured for Outlook Web App.
- ✓ If you are planning to use an ISA Server 2006 SP1 firewall to publish Exchange 2010 remote access then the authentication settings should be changed to enable both **Basic** and **Integrated Windows Authentication** to allow authentication delegation to work correctly.
- ✓ If you are not using ISA Server and plan to open a firewall port for direct access from the internet to the Client Access server for OWA then leave it configured to Forms-based Authentication.
- ✓ All other OWA default settings are fine for now. Click **OK** to apply the changes. A warning will appear to notify you that IIS must be restarted.
- ✓ Click **OK** to clear the warning, but there is no need to restart IIS yet. We're going to look at some other Client Access server configurations first.
- ✓ Repeat the same steps on the other internet-facing Client Access servers on the network to configure the Outlook Web App virtual directory.

One the above is done, on each of the branch office Client Access servers in your environment, configure the Basic and Integrated authentication options using the same steps above, but do not configure an External URL for those servers.

It's important to remember here that only internet-facing Client Access servers should be configured with an External URL on their virtual directories.

C.   CONFIGURING THE EXCHANGE CONTROL PANEL VIRTUAL DIRECTORY

- ✓ Select the **Exchange Control Panel** tab, right-click the ECP virtual directory and choose **Properties.**
- ✓ If you configured an external domain name during Exchange setup then the External URL for Outlook Web App will already be configured.
- ✓ Otherwise, configure the **External URL** with the same name as Outlook Web App.
- ✓ Select the **Authentication** tab and configure the same authentication methods as you are using for Outlook Web App.
- ✓ Click **OK** to apply the change.

Repeat the same steps on the other internet-facing Client Access servers on the network to configure the Exchange Control Panel virtual directory.

Then, on each of the branch office Client Access servers in your environment, configure the Basic and Integrated authentication options using the same steps above, but do not configure an External URL for those servers.

D.   CONFIGURING THE ACTIVESYNC VIRTUAL DIRECTORY

- ✓ If you configured an external domain name during Exchange setup then the External URL for ActiveSync will already be configured.
- ✓ Otherwise, select the **Exchange ActiveSync** tab, right-click the ActiveSync virtual directory and choose **Properties.**
- ✓ Configure the External URL with the external host name that you will use for mobile client connectivity. This is the name that was discovered during the planning phase and also a name that you included in the SSL certificate that was installed on the server.
- ✓ Click **OK** to apply the change.

Repeat the same steps on the other internet-facing Client Access servers on the network to configure the ActiveSync virtual directory.

E.   CONFIGURING THE OFFLINE ADDRESS BOOK VIRTUAL DIRECTORY

If you configured an external domain name during Exchange setup then the External URL for the Offline Address Book will already be configured.

- ✓ Otherwise, select the **Offline Address Book Distribution** tab, right-click the OAB virtual directory and choose **Properties.**
- ✓ Configure the External URL with the external host name for Outlook Address Book connectivity.
- ✓ Click OK to apply the change.
- ✓ Repeat the same steps on the other internet-facing Client Access servers on the network to configure the Offline Address Book virtual directory.
- ✓ The OAB virtual directory will also need an authentication configuration change if it is to be published externally using an ISA Server 2006 SP1 firewall. The authentication settings can only be configured using the Exchange Management Shell.
- ✓ Launch the Exchange Management Shell and run the following command for the OAB virtual directory on the internet-facing Client Access servers.

This is all a single-line command, and you should replace the server names to suit your environment.

```
[PS] C:\> Set-OabVirtualDirectory "HE-2K10-CH1\OAB (Default Web Site)"
-BasicAuthentication $true
[PS] C:\> Set-OabVirtualDirectory "HE-2K10-CH2\OAB (Default Web Site)"
-BasicAuthentication $true
```

F.   CONFIGURING THE EXCHANGE WEB SERVICES VIRTUAL DIRECTORY

The EWS virtual directory can only be configured using the Exchange Management Shell. Run the following command on the internet-facing Client Access servers using the external host name you chose for the SSL certificate earlier.

This is all a single-line command, and you should replace the server names to suit your environment:

```
[PS] C:\> Set-WebServicesVirtualDirectory -Identity "HE-2K10-CH1\EWS (Default web Site)" -
ExternalUrl https://mail.exchangeserverpro.net/EWS/Exchange.asmx
-BasicAuthentication:$true
    [PS] C:\> Set-WebServicesVirtualDirectory -Identity "HE-2K10-CH2\EWS (Default web Site)" -
                        ExternalUrl https://mail.exchangeserverpro.net/EWS/Exchange.asmx
-BasicAuthentication:$true
```

For additional client access server configurations at this stage, exchange admins should first refer to the following link http://technet.microsoft.com/en-us/library/bb310763.aspx or search for the Microsoft KB number bb310763 in google.com.

This is important as only the internet facing client access servers need the above configuration.

CONFIGURING THE HUB TRANSPORT SERVERS

The Hub Transport servers are responsible for all email message transmission between Exchange mailboxes, and between your organization and the internet. All email messages sent or received in the organization will traverse a Hub Transport server, including emails sent between two mailboxes stored on the same mailbox database.

Now we will configure each of the Hub Transport services, however, if there are services that an exchange administrator does not plan to use in their own environment they should skip them.

A.   CONFIGURING THE DEFAULT RECEIVE CONNECTOR

- ✓ Each Hub Transport server is configured during setup with a pair of Receive Connectors.
- ✓ **Default <servername>** - this Receive Connector is for receiving SMTP communications on TCP port 25
- ✓ **Client <servername>** - this Receive Connector is for mail submissions from email clients such as IMAP and POP
- ✓ The Default Receive Connector is created with a secure-by-default configuration, and will not accept email from external servers or non-Exchange servers without a configuration change.
- ✓ On the internet-facing Hub Transport server launch the Exchange Management Console and navigate to **Server Configuration/Hub Transport**, then click on the name of the Hub Transport server that will be receiving internet email.
- ✓ Right-click the Default Receive Connector and choose **Properties.**
- ✓ On the **Permissions Group** tab tick the box for **Anonymous users**, and then click **OK** to apply the change.

If more there is more than one internet-facing Hub Transport server that will be receiving incoming internet email, then one must repeat the same steps on that server as well.

The Default Receive Connector on other Hub Transport servers within the organization does not need this configuration change, because Exchange servers sending email to each other are not doing so anonymously.

B.   CONFIGURING THE RELAY CONNECTOR

In most organizations some applications or devices require the ability to relay email through the Exchange servers. During the planning phase of this guide you should have identified these applications and devices (page 21).

The source IP addresses of applications and devices that integrate with Exchange using SMTP will need to be added to a Receive Connector that permits relay. Using the information in your planning worksheet make a list of those IP addresses that need to be allowed.

You can also discover this information by inspecting the existing relay connector configuration on the Exchange 2007 servers.

- ✓ On an Exchange 2007 server launch the Exchange Management Console and navigate to **Server Configuration/Hub Transport**, then click on the name of the Hub Transport server that hosts the relay connector.

- ✓ Right-click the relay connector and choose **Properties**.

- ✓ Select the **Network tab** to see the list of remote IP addresses that are permitted to relay through this Receive Connector.

If there are only a few IP addresses one could just manually create the new relay connector on the Exchange 2010 server and enter the remote IP addresses one at a time however we can also use the EMC to do the same.

I will give a set of Power Shell Commands to get the job done, off course with a few changes to suit your environment in each of the commands given below.

```
[PS] C:\>$ips = (Get-ReceiveConnector "HO-EX2007-HT1\Relay HO-EX2007-HT1").RemoteIPRanges
```

Then run the following command to create the new relay connector on the Exchange 2010 Hub Transport server…

```
[PS] C:\>New-ReceiveConnector -Name "Relay HE-2K10-CH1" –Server HE-2K10-CH1" -Usage Custom -
AuthMechanism ExternalAuthoritative -PermissionGroups ExchangeServers -Bindings 0.0.0.0:25 -
RemoteIPRanges $ips
Identity                Bindings        Enabled
--------                --------        -------
HE-2K10-CH1\Relay HE-2K10-CH1 {0.0.0.0:25} True
```

That simple two-step process will migrate the relay connector from Exchange 2007 to Exchange 2010. Just be aware that any changes made to the Exchange 2007 relay connector won't automatically be changed on the Exchange 2010 relay connector, and vice versa. It is recommended that you maintain some change control over the two relay connectors while your migration project is still running.

Relay connectors such as this tend to be site-specific, so you should also check the other sites in your Exchange organization to see whether they have their own relay connectors configured on local Hub Transport servers.

CONFIGURING THE MAILBOX SERVERS

The Mailbox servers are responsible for hosting the mailbox and public folder databases for the organization.

Now we will go to the next step of configuring each of the Mailbox servers. Again I would recommend skipping sections for services that you do not plan to use in your own environment.

If you installed your Mailbox servers without using the command line options for specifying the correct database and log file locations then change those now to their correct folder paths to avoid further issues.

Search for the Microsoft KB on Google or see the following article for the required steps to move the exchange 2010 database folder.

```
Assuming that the database name is HE-05, here is the Exchange PS command
that we can use to move it.

Move-DatabasePath -Identity 'HE-05' -EdbFilePath 'E:\Data\HE-05\HE-05.edb' -
LogFolderPath 'D:\Data\HE-05'
```

A.   CREATING ADDITIONAL MAILBOX DATABASES

Depending on how you intend to distribute mailboxes across the available databases on your Exchange servers, this is the right time to create any additional mailbox databases that your organization needs.

You might choose to distribute mailboxes according to:
• Geographic location
• Corporate division or department
• Mailbox type (e.g. user, shared, resource)
• Surnames of mailbox users
• Storage quotas required by users (since these are set at the database level)

  ✓ To create a new mailbox database open the Exchange Management Console and navigate to Organization Configuration/Mailbox.
  ✓ In the Actions pane click on **New Mailbox Database**.
  ✓ Enter a name for the new mailbox database, and then click on Browse.

- ✓ Choose the mailbox server that you want to host the new mailbox database, and then click **OK**.
- ✓ Click **Next**, then enter the paths to the database and transaction log files.
- ✓ Note that the **Mount this database** option is ticked by default. This is fine however it is not unusual for a newly created database to fail to mount the first time. This is usually due to Active Directory replication delays. If the new database fails to mount just wait for Active Directory to fully replicate before you manually mount the database.
- ✓ Click on **Next** to continue, and then **New** to create the database.

This process must be repeated for each mailbox database that you need to create in your organization.

B. CREATING PUBLIC FOLDER DATABASES

You need a public folder database on Exchange Server 2010 if you:

- Have existing public folder content that you want to retain after the transition to Exchange Server 2010
- Have Outlook 2003 clients on the network.

- ✓ Launch the Exchange Management Console and navigate to **Organization Configuration/Mailbox**.
- ✓ In the Actions pane click on **New Mailbox Database.**
- ✓ Enter a name for the new public folder database, and then click on **Browse.**
- ✓ Choose the mailbox server that you want to host the new public folder database, and then click **OK**.
- ✓ Click **Next**, then enter the paths to the database and transaction log files.
- ✓ Note that the **Mount this database** option is ticked by default. As with mailbox databases this is fine however it is not unusual for a newly created database to fail to mount the first time. This is usually due to Active Directory replication delays. If the new database fails to mount just wait for Active Directory to fully replicate before you manually mount the database Active Directory replication delays. If the new database fails to mount just wait for Active Directory to fully replicate before you manually mount the database.

This process must be repeated for each public folder database that you need to create in your organization.

C. CONFIGURING MAILBOX DATABASE SETTINGS

- ✓ Each mailbox database has some settings that you should review and modify to suit your environment.
- ✓ Open the Exchange Management Console and navigate to **Organization Configuration/Mailbox**. Right-click the first mailbox database and select **Properties**.
- ✓ Select the **Limits** tab and review the storage limits that will be enforced for mailboxes that are on this mailbox database.

The default storage limits for Exchange 2010 allow for a 2 GB mailbox size. You may wish to decrease or increase this to meet your organization's requirements, or to match the Exchange 2007 mailbox storage quotas.

Important Information: *Exchange Server 2010 databases have significantly lower disk performance load than Exchange 2007, so it is capable of handling larger mailboxes than previous versions of Exchange.*

- ✓ Next select the Client Settings tab, and confirm that the correct public folder database and offline address book is configured for mailbox users on this database.
- ✓ Click OK to apply any changes, and then repeat this process for all of the Exchange 2010 mailbox databases in your organization.

Each public folder database also has some settings that you should review.

1. Open the Exchange Management Console and navigate to **Organization Configuration/Mailbox**
2. Right-click the first public folder database and select **Properties**
3. Select the **Limits** tab and review the storage limits that are configured on the public folder database. You may need to adjust these to match the settings that you recorded on your planning worksheet earlier in this guide.
4. Click **OK** to apply any changes that you made, and then repeat this process for all of the Exchange 2010 public folder databases in your organization.

D.   CONFIGURING PUBLIC FOLDER REPLICAS

The full migration of public folder replicas will be handled later in this guide; however there are a few special considerations that need to be dealt with now.

If you have Outlook 2003 clients in your environment then they will rely on public folders for the Offline Address Book and the Schedule+ Free/Busy data. For this data to be available to them you need to manually configure replicas for those special public folders.

1. On an Exchange 2010 server open the Exchange Management Console. In the **Toolbox** open the **Public Folder Management Console.**
2. In the **Actions** pane click on **Connect to Server.**
3. In the Connect to Server dialog box click on **Browse.**
4. Choose a public folder server from the list and click **OK.**
5. Click **Connect** to make a connection to the public folder server.
6. Expand the System Public Folders and then click on Offline Address Book. In the middle pane right click the Offline Address Book used by your organization (usually the Default Offline Address Book) and select **Properties**.
7. On the **Replication** tab click on the **Add** button.
8. Select the Exchange 2010 public folder instances that you wish to replicate the Offline Address Book to, and then click **OK.**
9. Click **OK** to apply the changes.
10. Next, click on the Schedule+ Free Busy folder and in the middle pane right-click the free/busy object and choose **Properties**.
11. On the **Replication** tab complete the same steps as before to add the Exchange 2010 public folder servers as replicas of the folder.

12. You will now need to wait for the public folder replication interval to pass before you will see these changes take full effect.

CONFIGURING THE DATABASE AVAILABILITY GROUP

After the Mailbox servers and mailbox databases have been created you can proceed with creating a Database Availability Group. If you are not planning to deploy a DAG in your environment you can skip this section.

A. CREATING THE DATABASE AVAILABILITY GROUP

Log on to one of the Exchange 2010 Mailbox servers that will be a member of the DAG and launch the Exchange Management Console. Navigate to **Organization Configuration/Mailbox** and choose **New Database Availability Group** from the Action Pane.

When the **New Database Availability Group** wizard starts give the DAG a **name**, specify the **Witness server**, and also specify the **file path** for the Witness server to use. The witness server is typically another.

Exchange 2010 server in the same Active Directory site as the DAG members, for example a Hub Transport server.

Click on the **New** button to create the new Database Availability Group, and then click **Finish** to close the wizard.

B. ADDING DATABASE AVAILABILITY GROUP MEMBERS

Next we need to add members to the Database Availability Group. Right-click the newly created DAG and choose Manage Database Availability Group Membership.

Click the **Add** button and select the Mailbox servers that you wish to make members of the DAG.

Click the **Manage** button to commence adding the Mailbox servers to the DAG. This involves the wizard automatically installing and configuring Windows Failover Clustering on the servers, so it can take a few minutes to finish.

C. CONFIGURE DATABASE AVAILABILITY GROUP NETWORKING

1. After the DAG members have been added the next step is to configure the DAG networking.
2. Right-click the newly created Database Availability Group and choose **Properties.**

3. Select the **IP Addresses** tab, click the **Add** button and add a static IP address for the Database Availability Group.
4. Click **OK** and then **OK** again to apply the change and close the Properties of the DAG.
5. You will notice that the Database Availability Group has been automatically configured with DAG networks for the subnets that the DAG members have network interfaces connected to.
6. Open the **Properties** of each DAG network and configure them with meaningful names.
7. If you have configured your network to have dedicated replication networks for the DAG then you can consider disabling replication on the DAG network that is intended for MAPI communications (i.e. client connections).

Tip: Disabling replication on the client-facing network does not mean that replication can never occur over that network. It simply means that replication will not occur over that client-facing network until all other dedicated replication networks have failed. So it is safe to disable replication on the client-facing network when dedicated replication networks exist.

D. ADDING MAILBOX DATABASE COPIES TO DAG MEMBERS

With the Database Availability Group established and the networking configured you can now add mailbox database copies to other DAG members.

In the Exchange Management Console navigate to Organization Configuration/Mailbox and choose the Database Management tab. Right-click a mailbox database and select Add Mailbox Database Copy. If you do not see that option immediately available for a mailbox database that is on one of the Mailbox server you added to the DAG then click Refresh in the Action Pane and try again.

1. Click the **Browse** button and choose the Mailbox server to add the database copy to.

2. Click the **Add** button to add the mailbox database copy and then click **Finish** to close the wizard.
3. The Exchange servers will now commence seeding the replica servers with an up to date copy of the database and all of the current transaction log files. Depending on the amount of data to be replicated this may take some time to complete.

4. Repeat the same process for any other mailbox databases you wish to add database copies for.
5. Configuration of the Exchange Server 2010 Database Availability Group is now complete.

Tip: You may notice in the properties of the database copies the Activation Preference setting. Basically this setting influences the order in which you want database copies to activate if there is a server down. For example if the server with activation preference 1 is down, but 2 and 3 are up, then the database may activate on the server with preference 2, assuming the "Best Copy Selection" process determines that is the best candidate to be mounted.
This preference number is also referenced by scripts that can automatically rebalance the active database copies across an entire DAG.
Configure the activation preferences to suit how you would like the active database copies distributed under normal, healthy operations.

Configuring Co-Existence

Up until now the Exchange 2010 servers have been installed and configured mostly in isolation from the production environment. But now we are approaching the stage of the migration project where the Exchange 2010 servers begin to perform production roles, such as message routing, remote access, and hosting mailboxes.

This period is referred to as the "co-existence" period.

For some organizations a co-existence period is not necessary, because they are small enough that 100% of the services and data on Exchange 2007 can be migrated across to Exchange 2010 within a single outage window.

For example a small business with just a few dozen, small mailboxes could perform the entire migration in a single weekend with no business hours impact. Such organizations can skip the co-existence phase if they wish to, which reduces the amount of configuration work required.

However for the rest of us a co-existence period is usually necessary, which means there are some important configurations to put in place first before any production services or data are migrated to Exchange 2010.

Establishing the Legacy Namespace

The legacy namespace is the name that will be used by Exchange 2007 mailbox users to access Outlook Web Access after the remote access namespace is transitioned to the internet-facing Exchange 2010 Client Access server.

What this means is that Outlook Web Access/App connections are first made to the Client Access server. Exchange 2010 mailbox users are proxied as normal to the appropriate Mailbox server. However Exchange 2007 mailbox users are redirected to the legacy namespace instead.

Some people find the legacy namespace to be a confusing topic. In effect the legacy namespace is simply another DNS name, published via ISA Server or another firewall, that legacy (Exchange 2007) mailbox users are redirected to for Outlook Web Access.

In this simple example the OWA namespace is published via an ISA server to the Exchange 2010 Client Access server. An Exchange 2010 mailbox user is able to connect to their mailbox as you would expect.

However when an Exchange 2007 mailbox user makes a connection to the Exchange 2010 Client Access server they are redirected to the legacy URL instead, which the ISA server publishes to the Exchange 2007 Client Access server. They are then able to connect to the Exchange 2007 mailbox. The redirection can be configured to occur completely silently thanks to ISA Server's single sign-on capabilities.

CREATING THE LEGACY DNS RECORD

You may recall choosing a legacy name during the creation of the SSL certificate request earlier in this guide.

The legacy name can be anything you like however the name that is commonly chosen is "legacy", so in this example scenario **legacy.chetanpawar.com**.

Create a DNS record for the legacy name in your public DNS zone. If you are using split DNS you should also create the record in your internal DNS zone, pointing to the internet-facing Exchange 2007 Client Access server.

The public IP address that the DNS record is created for can be the same as the public IP address of your primary remote access name (e.g. mail.exchangeserverpro.net) if you are using ISA Server 2006 to publish Exchange remote access. ISA Server is capable of publishing the different names to different internal servers using the same web listener.

If you are using a different firewall or a simple NAT router then you may need to configure the legacy namespace on a separate public IP address than the primary OWA namespace.

Tip: If you are using split DNS take a look at how your existing OWA public name is configured in your internal DNS zone. If it uses the public IP then do the same with your legacy name, however if it uses the internal IP then you should configure the legacy name to the internal IP as well for the internal DNS zone.

CONFIGURING THE OWA VIRTUAL DIRECTORY FOR LEGACY REDIRECTION

The OWA Virtual Directory on each of the internet-facing Exchange 2010 Client Access servers must be configured with the legacy URL to redirect users to.

Open the Exchange Management Shell and run the Set-OWAVirtualDirectory command with the following parameters:
- **-Identity** is the name of the OWA Virtual Directory being modified
- **-Exchange2003URL** is the legacy URL to redirect Exchange 2007 mailbox users to (yes, even though the parameter is named Exchange2003URL).

```
[PS] C:\>Set-OwaVirtualDirectory -Identity "HE-2K10-CH1\owa (Default Web Site)" -
Exchange2003Url https://legacy.chetanpawar.com/owa
[PS] C:\>Set-OwaVirtualDirectory -Identity "HE-2K10-CH2\owa (Default Web Site)" -
Exchange2003Url https://legacy.chetanpawar.com/owa
```

After the change to the OWA virtual directories we need to restart IIS for the change to take effect. To restart IIS log on to each server and run the following command.

```
[PS] C:\>iisreset
Attempting stop...
```

```
Internet services successfully stopped
Attempting start...
Internet services successfully restarted
```

ASSIGNING THE SSL CERTIFICATE TO EXCHANGE SERVER 2007

The internet-facing Exchange 2007 Client Access server needs to be configured with a new SAN certificate that includes the legacy namespace. This is so that remote access connections to the legacy namespace, both from inside and outside of the network, can occur over SSL without any certificate errors or warnings.

In the SSL planning section of this guide (page 23) I explained that for this example I'll be provisioning a new SSL certificate on the internet-facing Exchange 2007 Client Access server that includes:
- The fully qualified domain name of the server HO-EX2007-CA1.chetanpawar.com
- Public names, such as mail. chetanpawar.com and autodiscover. chetanpawar.com
- The legacy namespace of legacy. chetanpawar.com

The first step to provision this certificate is to create the certificate request. Exchange 2007 doesn't have a nice graphical wizard for this; we need to use the Exchange Management Shell. To save time I suggest that we use Digicert's Exchange 2007 CSR Tool which is available at: https://www.digicert.com/easy-csr/exchange2007.htm to generate the correct command syntax.

Download the CSR Tool
Fill out the Certificate Details form with the details you want for your certificate, and then click the Generate button.
The New-ExchangeCertificate command syntax will appear on the right-hand side of the page.
Copy the command text to the clipboard, and then on the internet-facing Exchange 2007 Client Access server open the Exchange Management Shell, paste in the command and press Enter to run it.

```
[PS] C:\>New-ExchangeCertificate -GenerateRequest -Path c:\mail_exchangeserverpr
o_net.csr -KeySize 2048 -SubjectName "c=au, s=Queensland, l=Brisbane, o=Exchange
Server Pro, ou=IT Services, cn=mail.exchangeserverpro.net" -DomainName autodisc
over.exchangeserverpro.net, ho-ex2007-ca1.exchangeserverpro.net, legacy.exchange
serverpro.net -PrivateKeyExportable $True
Thumbprint Services Subject
---------- -------- -------
DD20E360B8E1A9B37F472939C4FB9BA6C30AF367 ..... C=au, S=Queensland, L=B...
```

The command will create a certificate request file in the path specified by the –Path command line parameter. This is the file that will be submitted to the Certificate Authority you are using to issue the SSL certificate.

As with the SSL certificate you provisioned for Exchange 2010, although you can generate the certificate from a private Certificate Authority it is recommended to use a public Certificate Authority such as Digicert.

Whichever Certificate Authority you choose for your SSL certificates simply follow their instructions for submitting your certificate request and receiving the generated certificate from them.

When you've received the certificate file from your provider, copy it to the Exchange 2007 Client Access server and run the following command to import it.

```
[PS] C:\>Import-ExchangeCertificate -Path C:\certnew.cer
Thumbprint Services Subject
---------- -------- -------
4A785CE7F60890ED03C395783C3AE3917E90E117 ..... CN=mail.chetanp...
```

Now enable the new SSL certificate for use by Exchange services. You may wish to perform this change outside of business hours so that you can test it afterwards and reverse the change if you discover any problems. Use the same thumbprint that was shown when you ran the import command.

```
[PS]  C:\>Enable-ExchangeCertificate  4A785CE7F60890ED03C395783C3AE3917E90E117  -Se
rvices IIS
```

ASSIGNING THE SSL CERTIFICATE TO ISA SERVER

The ISA Server that publishes Exchange Server remote access must also be installed with a certificate so that it can respond to requests for both the primary namespace and the legacy namespace.

Although some organizations may wish to provision a completely separate SSL certificate for use on the ISA Server, it is common to simply export the SAN certificate used by the internet-facing Exchange 2010 Client Access servers and import it to the ISA Server.

1. On the Exchange 2010 Client Access server open the Exchange Management Console and navigate to **Server Configuration**.
2. Right-click the Exchange 2010 Certificate and choose **Export Exchange Certificate.**
3. Click the **Browse** button and choose a location and file name to save the exported certificate. Enter a password to protect the exported certificate, and then click **Export.**
4. **When the export operation has completed click the Finish button.**
5. Copy the exported certificate file to the local disk of the ISA Server.
6. On the ISA Server launch mmc.exe and click **File Add/Remove** Snap-in to add the Certificates snap-in to the console, choosing the Computer account context.
7. Choose **Local Computer** and then click **Finish, Close,** and **OK** to return to the console.
8. Right-click **Personal** and choose **All Tasks □ Import**.
9. Step through the Certificate Import Wizard choosing the certificate file that was copied from the Exchange Server 2010 server.
10. Enter the password that you used when the certificate was exported from Exchange Server 2010.
11. Place the certificate in the **Personal** certificate store.
12. Complete the wizard and confirm that the import was successful.
13. The imported certificate will now appear alongside the existing SSL certificate on the ISA Server.

14. After it has been imported on the ISA Server the next step is to configure the publishing rule to use the new certificate. You may wish to perform this task outside of business hours so that you can perform testing and reverse the change if a problem is found.
15. On the ISA Server launch the ISA Server Management console. In the **Firewall Policy** section locate the publishing rule for the Exchange 2007 server.
16. Double-click to open the **Properties** of the publishing rule. Select the **Listener** tab and then click **Properties**.
17. Select the **Certificates** tab, and then click **Select Certificate**.
18. From the list of SSL certificates choose the certificate that was imported from Exchange 2010, and then click **Select**.
19. Click **OK**, and then **OK** again. Finally, click on **Apply** to apply the changes to the ISA firewall rules.

You should now test your Exchange 2007 remote access (e.g. Outlook Web Access) to verify that the new certificate is working correctly with all of the changes that have just been made.

CONFIGURING THE ISA SERVER PUBLISHING RULE

When the ISA Server is reconfigured to publish Exchange remote access requests to the Exchange 2010 Client Access server it will still require a publishing rule in place for the legacy namespace to be published to the Exchange 2007 Client Access server.

The simplest way to create the publishing rule for the legacy namespace is to copy the existing rule, and then make just a few modifications to it.

In the ISA Server Management console navigate to the Firewall Policy section and then locate the existing Exchange 2007 publishing rule.

1. Right-click the publishing rule and then select **Copy.**
2. Right-click the publishing rule again and choose **Paste**. The copy of the publishing rule will appear in the list.
3. Double-click to open the **Properties** of the copied publishing rule. On the **General** tab give the rule a new name.
4. Select the **Public Name** tab, highlight the existing public name and click **Remove**.
5. Click on **Add** and enter the legacy name that you are using for your organization.
6. On the **To** tab of the rule change the name of the published site to match the legacy name.
7. Click Apply to apply the changes to the rule. Then while still on the **To** tab of the rule, click on the **Test Rule** button to test the changes.
8. The test results should be all successful before you proceed any further. If you have any tests that fail you should investigate and resolve those before committing the changes to the firewall.
9. Click **OK** to apply the changes to the rule. Then click **Apply** to apply the changes to the firewall.

Once again you should test your Exchange remote access to make sure that the changes that have been made have not caused a problem.

Configuring the ISA Server publishing rule for the legacy namespace is only a preparation task at this stage; it does not mean that remote access users will be connecting to that name yet. That cutover will be performed a little later on in the migration.

CONFIGURING APPLICATION AND DEVICE INTEGRATION

In the planning section of this guide we covered discovery of Exchange-integrated applications and devices within your organization.

Now it is time to configure the new Exchange Server 2010 servers to support those applications and devices.

For application integration it is recommended that you refer to the application vendor's documentation for any specific Exchange Server 2010 configurations that are required.

These may include:
- Service account mailboxes
- Delegation of Exchange permissions to service accounts
- Installation of agents directly onto the Exchange servers

One of the key Exchange-integrated applications in any environment is backup software. It is critical that you correctly configure and test your backup software with Exchange Server 2010 before you place the new servers into production.

For device integration this usually means SMTP relay access through the servers. You can refer to the section earlier on creating a Receive Connector for SMTP relay access.

Tip: Perform all of your application and device integration tasks before proceeding to the testing and pilot phases of the project, so that the testing scenarios cover all of your organization and end user requirements.

CHECKPOST 1:   All the below must be checked at this stage before proceeding for a successful migration

Before proceeding further with your Exchange Server 2010 project, ensure that you have:

- ✓ Provisioned adequate server hardware resources for Exchange Server 2010 to meet your organization's requirements.
- ✓ Prepared each new server with the correct operating system, name and network configuration for your organization.
- ✓ Prepared the Active Directory for Exchange Server 2010 by installing the schema updates.
- ✓ Installed each of the Exchange Server 2010 servers in your organization.

- ✓ Deployed SSL certificates for Exchange Server 2010.
- ✓ Entered the Exchange Server 2010 product key.
- ✓ Configured each Client Access server.
- ✓ Configured each Hub Transport server.
- ✓ Configured each Mailbox server.
- ✓ Configured co-existence.
- ✓ Configured application and device integration with Exchange Server 2010.

TESTING THE NEW EXCHANGE SERVER

Now that the new Exchange Server 2010 environment has been installed and configured we can proceed with the testing phase of the project.

CREATING TEST MAILBOXES ON EXCHANGE SERVER 2010 MAILBOX SERVERS

To perform the testing in this section we must first create some test user mailboxes on each of the Mailbox servers.

1. Launch the **Exchange Management Console** and navigate **Recipient Configuration/Mailbox**.
2. In the Actions pane click on **New Mailbox** to start the New Mailbox Wizard.
3. Select **User Mailbox** and click **Next** to continue.
4. Select **New user** and click **Next** to continue.
5. Enter the user information for the test mailbox. The OU to create the associated user account in is optional.
6. Tick the box to **Specify the mailbox database** and then click **Browse**.
7. Choose the mailbox database to create the new mailbox on, click **OK**, and then click **Next** to continue.
8. Do not create an archive at this time. Click **Next** to continue.
9. Confirm the information you have entered and then click **New** to create the new mailbox.
10. Repeat this process to create test mailboxes on each of the Exchange 2010 Mailbox servers in your organization, or if you're running a DAG you should create test mailboxes for every mailbox database as well.

Tip: Use the testing worksheet included with this guide to record the usernames and Mailbox servers for each of the test mailboxes you have created.

TESTING AUTODISCOVER AND AUTO-CONFIGURATION

If your users are using Outlook 2007 or 2010 you should test that Autodiscover and auto-configuration are working correctly.

To perform this test logon to a workstation that has Outlook 2007 or 2010 installed with the username and password of one of the test mailboxes you have created in the previous section.

1. Launch **Microsoft Outlook**, and click **Next** to move past the welcome dialog box.
2. Choose **Yes** to create a new email account, and click **Next** to continue.
3. Outlook should automatically detect the email address of the test user account.
4. Click **Next** to continue.
5. Outlook should then automatically configure the correct settings for the email account.
6. Click **Finish** to complete automatic configuration of Outlook. Repeat this process for each of the test mailboxes you have created so that Autodiscover is tested in all of your sites.

Tip: Use the testing worksheet to record the result of the Autodiscover and auto-configuration tests for each of your Mailbox servers.

TESTING OUTLOOK WEB APP

Although Outlook Web App is not yet published externally you should still test it internally to make sure that the logon format and proxy/redirection is working correctly.
You can determine the internal URL for Outlook Web App by checking the OWA virtual directory configuration of the Client Access server, and browsing to that URL in Internet Explorer.

I recommend testing OWA with the following mailbox users:

- An Exchange 2010 test mailbox that is on a database in the same site as the internet-facing Exchange 2010 Client Access server

- An Exchange 2010 test mailbox that is on a database in a different site to the internet-facing Exchange 2010 Client Access server

- An Exchange 2007 test mailbox that is on a database in the same site as the internet-facing Exchange 2010 Client Access server

- An Exchange 2007 test mailbox that is on a database in a different site to the internet-facing Exchange 2010 Client Access server

If successful, Exchange 2010 mailbox users will see the Exchange 2010 OWA interface.
Exchange 2007 mailbox users will be redirected to the legacy URL and will see the OWA 2007 interface.

Tip: Use the testing worksheet included with this guide to record the OWA tests that were performed, and the results of each one.

TESTING MAIL FLOW

Using the Exchange 2010 test mailboxes that you have created, as well as existing user mailboxes or test mailboxes on Exchange Server 2007 servers, test the internal and external email flow for the organization.

You can perform these tests simply by using Outlook and sending emails between each of the test mailboxes, as well as to and from an external mailbox.

For the internal test emails you can use delivery receipts to save some time confirming successful delivery of the test emails.

Tip: Use the testing worksheet included with this guide to record the email delivery tests that were performed, and the results of each one.

TESTING PUBLIC FOLDER ACCESS

If you are not using public folders in your organization you can skip this step.

At this stage of the project public folder content has not yet been replicated to the new Exchange Server 2010 Mailbox servers. However public folder access should still be functioning thanks to public folder referrals.

For each of the sites in your organization logon to a test mailbox and confirm that the expected level of public folder access is available. Depending on how you secure your public folders you may need to add the test mailbox user to a security group first.

Tip: Use the testing worksheet included with this guide to record the public folder tests performed as well as their results.

TESTING CALENDAR FREE/BUSY INFORMATION

One of the most important functions of Exchange for many businesses is calendar free/busy information for scheduling meetings, so this needs to be tested.

This is particularly important if you are still using any Outlook 2003 clients, which rely on public folders for Free/Busy information.

For each of the test mailboxes in your organization create a new meeting in Outlook and invite at least one other Exchange 2007 and Exchange 2010 mailbox user to confirm that their free/busy information is visible in the meeting request.

Tip: Use the testing worksheet included with this guide to record the Free/Busy tests performed as well as their results.

TESTING BACKUP AND RESTORE

A working backup and recovery capability for the new Exchange 2010 servers, particularly the Mailbox servers, is critical to your organization.

I recommend you test at a minimum the following operations:

- ✓ Manual and scheduled backup of servers databases (some backup products behave differently between manual and scheduled jobs)
- ✓ Restore of an entire mailbox database
- ✓ Restore of an individual mailbox or mailbox item
- ✓ Restore of an entire public folder database
- ✓ Restore of an individual public folder or public folder item

Tip: Use the testing worksheet included with this guide to record the backup and recovery tests performed as well as their results

CHECKPOST - 2: Check Before Proceeding Further for a Successful Migration

Before proceeding further with your Exchange Server 2010 project, ensure that you have:

- ✓ Created test mailboxes on each Exchange Server 2010 Mailbox server.
- ✓ Tested Autodiscover and auto-configuration for Outlook 2007 and 2010 clients.
- ✓ Tested Outlook Web App.
- ✓ Tested mail flow internal and external to the organization.
- ✓ Tested public folder access.
- ✓ Tested calendar Free/Busy information.
- ✓ Tested backup and restore of Exchange Server 2010.

MIGRATING TO EXCHANGE SERVER 2010

CLIENT ACCESS MIGRATION TO EXCHANGE SERVER 2010

Before migrating any pilot or production mailboxes the Client Access services (e.g. Outlook Web App and ActiveSync) need to be cut over from Exchange Server 2007 to Exchange Server 2010.

This change will often require a minor outage for these services, and it will bring the legacy namespace configuration into production for those organizations that have configured one for co-existence.
As such it is recommended to schedule this change for a time when it will cause the least business impact and to allow you time to test the changes and revert them if you encounter any problems.

This section of the guide demonstrates the migration scenario when ISA Server 2006 SP1 is used to publish Exchange remote access. If you are using another firewall product or NAT router then it is likely that all you need to do is change the NAT rule on your firewall or router from the Exchange 2007 Client Access server to the Exchange 2010 Client Access server.

The rest of this section then would not apply to you.

A.   EXPORTING THE EXISTING ISA SERVER FIREWALL POLICY

Before making any changes to the firewall rules it is recommended to export the current policy first. Log on to the ISA Server firewall and launch the **ISA Server Management** console.

- ✓ Right-click **Firewall Policy** and choose **Export**.
- ✓ Click **Next** to proceed past the welcome dialog of the Export Wizard. Tick the box to **Export confidential information**, and enter a password. Click **Next** to continue.
- ✓ Enter the full path for the file to store the exported data, and then click **Next** to continue.
- ✓ Click **Finish** to complete the Export Wizard.
- ✓ You now have a copy of the current firewall rules that you can use to roll back the changes if there are serious problems.

B.   MIGRATING CLIENT ACCESS SERVICES TO A SINGLE EXCHANGE 2010 CLIENT ACCESS SERVER

If you are migrating from a single Exchange 2007 Client Access server to a single Exchange 2010 Client Access server the fastest way to make the ISA Server changes is to simply modify your existing publishing rule.

If you are planning to publish a CAS Array instead then you can skip this section.

In the ISA Server Management console click on **Firewall Policy**, right-click on the existing Exchange 2007 publishing rule and select Properties.

- ✓ First, change the name to represent the new purpose of the rule.
- ✓ Select the **To** tab and change the **Computer name or IP address** to the name of the internet-facing Exchange 2010 Client Access server.
- ✓ Select the **Paths** tab and click the **Add** button to add a new path.
- ✓ Enter a new path of **/ecp/*** and click OK.
- ✓ Click the **Apply** button.
- ✓ Next, click the **Test Rule** button to test the rule before it is committed to the ISA Server configuration.
- ✓ If all of the tests are successful click the **Close** button to close the test results, click **OK** to close the properties of the publishing rule, and then click **Apply** to commit the changes to the Firewall Policy.

✓ Next, if you are using split DNS update the internal DNS record for your webmail name to point to the Exchange 2010 Client Access server.
✓ Finally, update the External URL of the OWA Virtual Directory on the Exchange 2007 Client Access server to match the legacy namespace that is now used to access it.

C.   MIGRATING CLIENT ACCESS SERVICES TO AN EXCHANGE 2010 CLIENT ACCESS SERVER ARRAY

If you are running multiple internet-facing Exchange 2010 Client Access servers configured in a CAS Array you can publish them with ISA Server 2006 as a web server farm.

If you are running a single internet-facing Client Access server in your environment you can skip this section.

The advantage of publishing multiple Client Access servers is that the ISA Server can provide load-balancing of external access that is service-aware; in other words it can be configured to detect when one of the Client Access servers is having a problem and automatically remove that server from the web server farm until it is healthy again.

In comparison, if you were to configure the ISA Server publishing rule to use the NLB virtual IP address of your Client Access Server Array it would be subject to limitations of NLB, such as that NLB is server-aware but not service-aware. In other words, an NLB cluster member has to experience a serious problem, not just a minor issue such as having problems with a single component, before the NLB cluster will stop trying to load-balance client traffic to that server.

Publishing the Exchange 2010 Client Access servers as a web server farm involves creating an entirely new publishing rule on the ISA Server firewall.

✓ In the ISA Server Management console right-click on **Firewall Policy** and select **New > Exchange Web Client Access Publishing Rule**.
✓ Give the new rule a meaningful name, then click **Next**.
✓ Set the **Exchange version** to Exchange Server 2007 (this will work for Exchange 2010 as well), then tick the box for **Outlook Web Access**. Click **Next** to continue.
✓ Select **Publish a server farm of load balanced Web servers**, then click **Next** to continue.
✓ Select **Use SSL to connect to the published Web server or server farm**, and then click **Next** to continue.
✓ Enter the **Internal site name**, which is the name that internal users would type in their web browser to access Outlook Web App from inside the network. Click **Next** to continue.
✓ Now we need to create a server farm in ISA Server. Click the **New** button to begin.
✓ Give the new server farm a meaningful name, then click **Next** to continue.
✓ Now we need to add servers to the server farm. Click on **Add** to begin.
✓ Enter the names of each of your internet-facing Exchange 2010 Client Access servers one at a time.

✓ After you've added each of your internet-facing Exchange 2010 Client Access servers click on **Next** to continue.

- ✓ As described earlier when ISA Server publishes a web server farm it can be configured to be service-aware. You can achieve this by leaving the **Server Farm Connectivity Monitoring** set to the default setting of **Send an HTTP/HTTPS Get request**, so that ISA will actually verify that the Client Access server is not only up but also responding to web requests.
- ✓ Click **Next** to continue, then click **Finish** to complete the new server farm.
- ✓ If this was the first server farm you've created in ISA Server you may be prompted to allow the ISA Server to connect to the servers that it is configured to use connectivity verifiers for.
- ✓ Click **Yes** to accept that change to the system policy.
- ✓ Select the server farm that you've just created and click **Next** to continue.
- ✓ Enter the public name that your users will be using to connect to Outlook Web App, and click **Next** to continue.
- ✓ Select the web listener that you use for the existing Exchange 2007 publishing rule, and then click **Next** to continue.

In this guide we'll be using a single publishing rule for all Exchange 2010 remote access, so **Basic Authentication** is the delegation type that is chosen.

- ✓ Click **Next** to continue.
- ✓ Leave the user sets configured for **All Authenticated Users** and click **Next** to continue.
- ✓ Before completing the publishing rule wizard click on the **Test Rule** button.
- ✓ All of the tests should be successful if there are no underlying issues. If you do see any failed tests then click on those results for an explanation of why they failed, and take corrective action before you continue.
- ✓ Otherwise, click on **Close** and then **Finish**.

The web publishing rule is not yet completely configured, so do not apply the firewall configuration changes just yet.

Tip: In this demonstration a single ISA Server publishing rule will be configured for all of the Exchange 2010 services. If your organization needs has requirements that can't be met with a single rule then you may need to create multiple publishing rules instead.

- ✓ Right-click the web publishing rule and select **Properties**.
- ✓ On the **Public Name** tab click **Add** and add the Autodiscover name. This is optional; some organizations prefer not to publish Autodiscover externally.
- ✓ Select the **Paths** tab. There are several additional paths that need to be added here.
- ✓ The following paths need to be added to the publishing rule:
    - **/ecp/*** for the Exchange Control Panel
    - **/Autodiscover/*** for the Autodiscover service
    - **/EWS/*** for Exchange Web Services
    - **/Microsoft-Server-Activesync/*** for mobile device access
    - **/rpc/*** for Outlook Anywhere
    - **/OAB/*** for Offline Address Book access
- ✓ To add a path click on the **Add** button.
- ✓ Enter the path and click **OK** to add it to the list.
- ✓ Repeat this process for each of the paths that need to be added.
- ✓ Click **Apply**, and then click **Test Rule** to test the publishing rule for the new changes.

Again, all of the tests should be successful if there are no underlying issues. If you do see any failed tests then click on those results for an explanation of why they failed, and take corrective action before you continue.

- ✓ Click **Close** and then click **OK** to apply the changes to the web publishing rule.
- ✓ Right-click the existing Exchange 2007 publishing rule and select **Disable**.
- ✓ Click on **Apply** to commit the changes to the firewall configuration.

Next, if you are using split DNS update the internal DNS record for your webmail name to point to the Exchange 2010 CAS Array virtual IP address.

Finally, update the External URL of the OWA Virtual Directory on the Exchange 2007 Client Access server to match the legacy namespace that is now used to access it.

C.   COPYING THE EXCHANGE 2007 OWA RESOURCE FOLDER TO EXCHANGE 2010

Some of the CAS proxying and redirection scenarios will work without any further configuration, however there is one specific scenario that will not work without taking this additional step.

When the internet-facing Client Access server is Exchange 2010, and it proxies the OWA connection to an Exchange 2007 Client Access server in a different AD Site for a mailbox user in that AD Site, it will fail with the following error message:-

The mailbox you're trying to access isn't currently available. If the problem continues, contact your helpdesk.

The Exchange 2010 Client Access server that attempts to proxy the connection will also log this error in the Application Event Log.

```
Log Name: Application
Source: MSExchange OWA
Date: 1/5/2012 10:14:13 PM
Event ID: 46
Task Category: Proxy
Level: Error
Keywords: Classic
User: N/A
Computer: HE-2K10-CH1.exchangeserverpro.net
Description:
Client Access server "https://mail.exchangeserverpro.net/owa", running Exchange version
"14.1.323.3", is proxying Outlook Web App traffic to Client Access server "br-ex2007-
caht.exchangeserverpro.net", which runs Exchange version "8.3.83.4". To ensure reliable
interoperability, the proxying Client Access server needs to be running a newer version of
Exchange than the Client Access server it is proxying to. If the proxying Client Access server
is running a newer version of Exchange than the Client Access server it is proxying to, the
proxying Client Access server needs to have an Outlook Web App resource folder (for example,
"&lt;Exchange Server installation path&gt;)\ClientAccess\owa\8.0.498.0" that contains all the
same versioned resource files as the Client Access server it is proxying to. If you will be
running Outlook Web App proxying with mismatched server versions, you can manually copy this
```

resource folder to the proxying Client Access server. After you copy this resource folder to the proxying Client Access server, you need to restart IIS before proxying will work.

The solution is explained in the event log entry. Simply copy the OWA resource folder from the Exchange 2007 server to each of the internet-facing Exchange 2010 Client Access servers.

Then, on the Exchange 2010 Client Access servers restart IIS.

```
C:\Users\administrator.ESPNET>iisreset
Attempting stop...
Internet services successfully stopped
Attempting start...
Internet services successfully restarted
```

D.   TESTING THE EXCHANGE SERVER 2010 PUBLISHING RULE

Now that the ISA Server changes have been made they need to be tested. I recommend you perform the following tests:

For an Exchange 2007 mailbox user in each site:
- ✓ Outlook Web Access
- ✓ ActiveSync
- ✓ RPC over HTTPS

For an Exchange 2010 mailbox user in each site:
- ✓ Outlook Web App
- ✓ Exchange Control Panel (the Options area of OWA)
- ✓ ActiveSync
- ✓ Outlook Anywhere
- ✓ Autodiscover

You can perform these tests using a web browser, Outlook client, and ActiveSync mobile device from outside of your firewall.

However if you do not have an external connection or compatible device available to you Microsoft has created an online testing tool called the Exchange Remove Connectivity Analyzer that you can use instead. This tool can be downloaded from: https://www.testexchangeconnectivity.com/

EMAIL ROUTING MIGRATION TO EXCHANGE SERVER 2010

There are two parts to the migration of email routing to Exchange Server 2010:
- ✓ External email routing (email between your organization and external parties)
- ✓ Internal email routing (email between users, applications and devices on your network)

A.   MIGRATING EXTERNAL EMAIL ROUTING TO EXCHANGE SERVER 2010

The routing of email traffic in and out of the organization needs to be migrated from the current Exchange Server 2007 Hub Transport server to the Exchange Server 2010 Hub Transport server.

In the planning section of this guide you investigated your email routing topology to determine the inbound and outbound email path. Depending on the topology in your organization changing the email path may involve:

- ✓ Modifying firewall access rules or NAT rules
- ✓ Changing routing configurations on an external email security service
- ✓ Changing routing configurations on an internal smart host

In this scenario the ISA Server publishes incoming SMTP traffic to the Exchange 2007 Hub Transport server in the internet-facing AD site, and this needs to be changed to the Exchange 2010 Hub Transport server at the internet-facing site.

If you want to provide a highly available inbound SMTP route for external emails there are a few ways you can go about it.

The first is to use multiple MX records in your public DNS zone. If you want them to be load-balanced (to a degree) then use equal preference MX records. Alternatively if you'd prefer they operate in a primary/secondary manner use different preferences for the MX records.

Using multiple MX records will require you to have multiple public IP addresses so that each one can be NATed (or published by ISA Server) to a different Hub Transport server.

Another option is to use a load balancer to distribute the incoming SMTP connections. This can be placed inside the firewall and will work even if you have only one public IP address.

Note that if you plan to use load balancing for incoming SMTP traffic to Hub Transport servers there are some specific guidelines from Microsoft that you need to follow to be a supported configuration, such as configuring additional Receive Connectors.

During this experiment we are going to publish incoming external SMTP traffic to just one of the Exchange 2010 Hub Transport servers.

Tip: If your firewall restricts outbound SMTP as well you should update the firewall rules to allow the Exchange 2010 Hub Transport servers to make outbound SMTP connections.

1. Launch the **ISA Server Management** console and navigate to the **Firewall Policy**.
2. Right-click the existing SMTP Server publishing rule and choose **Properties.**
3. Select the **To** tab and change the network address to the IP address of the internet-facing Hub Transport server.
4. Click **OK**, and then click **Apply** to commit the changes to the ISA Firewall Policy.
5. Next we need to configure outbound email routing. This involves the creation of a Send Connector for Exchange Server 2010.

6. Launch the **Exchange Management Console** and navigate to **Organization Configuration/Hub Transport**.
7. Select the **Send Connectors** tab. The existing Send Connector for Exchange 2007 should be visible.
8. Right-click the Send Connector and choose **Properties.**
9. On the **Source Server** tab highlight the Exchange 2007 Hub Transport server and click the delete button.
10. Next, click on the **Add** button and select the Exchange 2010 Hub Transport servers that you want to use for sending outgoing external email. Click **OK** to add them to the Source Server list.
11. Click **OK** again to apply the changes and close the properties of the Send Connector.

Tip: If your firewall also restricts outbound SMTP access then add a rule to allow the Exchange Server 2010 Hub Transport server to connect out through the firewall on TCP port 25 (SMTP).

Now it is time to test the changes that have been made to inbound and outbound email routing. I recommend you perform the following tests:

- From an Exchange 2007 test mailbox in each site send email to and from an external email address

- From an Exchange 2010 test mailbox in each site send email to and from an external email address

Inspect the message headers of the test emails to verify that they went through the correct servers.

B.   MIGRATING INTERNAL EMAIL ROUTING TO EXCHANGE SERVER 2010

Internal applications and devices that use Exchange for SMTP connectivity need to be migrated to the Exchange 2010 Hub Transport server.

The setup of a Receive Connector that permits relaying was demonstrated on page 121 of this guide.

Depending on the applications and devices in your environment there can be different ways to perform this migration step:

✓ For environments that use a DNS alias to configure SMTP properties of applications and devices, update the DNS alias to point to the Exchange 2010 Hub Transport server

✓ For applications and devices that only accept IP addresses in the SMTP configuration, update those with the new IP address to use.

In preparation for decommissioning the Exchange 2007 servers, on each Receive Connector that is used for application relay enable protocol logging so that any unknown applications and devices that are still using the server for SMTP relay can be identified later.

To enable protocol logging; open the **Properties** of the relay connector on the Exchange 2007 Hub Transport server and set the **Protocol logging level** to **Verbose**.

The longer this logging occurs the better the chances that you will capture all relaying IP addresses.

PERFORMING A PILOT MAILBOX MIGRATION

Before proceeding with the full production mailbox migration it is useful to migrate a small pilot group first. This will help identify any issues that may arise during the bulk mailbox migrations.

A pilot group also helps learn how long the total mailbox migration is likely to take. Mailbox moves can run anywhere between 500mb/hr to 3Gb/hr depending on factors such as the source server hardware and network conditions.

A pilot group only needs to be as large as is necessary to form an adequate representative sample of your user population. I recommend your pilot group be made up of:

- Reasonably techies who can notice and report unexpected changes or errors caused by the migration.
- At least one user from each site or department in the organization
- At least one user of each Outlook version used on the network
- At least one mobile device user

Before you move any mailboxes it is worth verifying that your Exchange 2010 mailbox databases have the correct RPC Client Access Server attribute set.

To check this open an Exchange Management Shell window on one of your Exchange 2010 servers and run the following command.

```
[PS] C:\>get-mailboxdatabase | ft name,rpcclientaccessserver -auto
Name RpcClientAccessServer
---- ---------------------
MB-HE-01 outlook.chetanpawar.com
MB-HE-02 outlook. chetanpawar.com
MB-BR-01 BR-2K10-CH chetanpawar.com
MB-HE-03 outlook. chetanpawar.com
```

Verify that each your mailbox databases have the RpcClientAccessServer that you're expecting. For mailbox databases in sites where you have a CAS Array configured it should be the name of the CAS Array. For sites with a single Client Access server it should be the name of that Client Access server. If you need to modify any of them use the Set-MailboxDatabase cmdlet.

```
[PS] C:\>Set-MailboxDatabase MB-HE-01 -RpcClientAccessServer outlook.chetanpawar.com
```

Mailbox move requests are initiated using the Exchange 2010 management tools.

1. Launch the Exchange Management Console and navigate to **Recipient Configuration/Mailbox**.
2. Hold the CTRL key to select multiple mailboxes to move as a pilot group.
3. In the Actions pane click on **New Local Move Request**.

In this example all of the mailboxes selected will be moved to the same target mailbox database.
4. Click the **Browse** button to choose a target mailbox database.

5. Select the mailbox database to move the pilot group to and then click **OK**. Click **Next** to continue.
6. On the Move Settings dialog you'll notice the option to suspend moves when they are ready to complete. This option allows you to more precisely manage the timeframe in which the user is unable to access their mailbox, **thanks to a new feature of Exchange Server 2010 known as online mailbox moves.**

During an online mailbox move from Exchange 2007 SP2 to Exchange 2010 the end user is not locked out of the mailbox for the full duration of the move. Instead, the Exchange server performs the move and then only at the final stage does the end user get locked out for the move request to be completed.

This can dramatically shorten the amount of time that the user mailbox, particular larger mailboxes, is unavailable during the migration.

If you choose to suspend the move when it is ready for completion you can begin the mailbox move request at any time, and then have it sit in a suspended state until you are ready for it to be completed.

For this pilot migration example we will check the box to suspend the moves to demonstrate this process. However if you wish to have the move requests continue to completion on their own do not check the box.

7. Review the list of mailboxes that will be moved and then click **New** to create the move requests.
8. Click **Finish** to close the wizard.
9. The move requests are created and will be processed by an Exchange 2010 Client Access server. You can view the status of the move requests in the Exchange Management Console under **Recipient Configuration/Move Request**.
10. Right-click a move request and choose **Properties** to see the status of that move request.
11. When the move request is in this suspended state the user can still continue to access their mailbox on the original server. You can then notify them of the time you will be completing the move request, at which point they will be locked out of the mailbox and will need to restart Outlook afterwards.
12. When you are ready simply right-click on the move request and choose **Complete Move Request**. You can also hold the CTRL key to select multiple move requests and complete them all at once.
13. Again you can monitor the status of the move requests in the Exchange Management Console.
14. If the end users are still connected with Outlook they will see a message similar to this, and will need to restart Outlook to connect to their mailbox on the Exchange 2010 server.
15. Complete all of your planned pilot migrations and then allow time for those users to perform testing before you migrate any more mailboxes.

PLANNING THE PRODUCTION MAILBOX MIGRATIONS

After the pilot mailbox migration has been successfully completed you can use the results to plan the remaining migrations.

✓ How many mailboxes you move at a time will depend on these factors:

✓ The size of the mailboxes. The Exchange Profile Analyzer report generated during the planning phase of the project (page 7) will tell you the average mailbox size, and you can also get exact mailbox sizes from Exchange Management Shell.

✓ The speed at which data is able to be moved between the servers (*use the pilot migration results to estimate this*).

✓ The hours of the day those are available for moves to occur without impacting the business.

✓ The size of the transaction log volumes on the Exchange 2010 Mailbox servers.

✓ The last point there is of particular importance. Mailbox migrations generate a large amount of transaction logging on the server that the mailboxes are being moved to. This means that there is a risk of the transaction log volume running out of free disk space, which will cause the mailbox databases to dismount.

There are two strategies that can be used to mitigate this risk:
1. Keep the mailbox migration batches small, and use backups to truncate the logs at the end of each migration.
2. Enable circular logging on the mailbox databases.

For standalone Mailbox servers the first option is the best and is recommended. The second (circular logging) creates new risks and should only be used if absolutely necessary. If circular logging is used then

I strongly recommend you perform a backup of the mailbox databases immediately after a migration, and disable circular logging again.

However, if you are have deployed a Database Availability Group for your Exchange 2010 Mailbox servers then you can safely enable circular logging, because for DAG members it operates in a different way than for standalone Mailbox servers.

For DAG members circular logging is referred to as "continuous replication circular logging" (or CRCL). In CRCL log files are not deleted until they are safely replicated and replayed on each member of the DAG.

PERFORMING THE PRODUCTION MAILBOX MIGRATIONS

Mailbox moves are initiated using the Exchange 2010 management tools. The moves can be initiated using either the Exchange Management Console or the Exchange Management Shell. There are only a few minor differences between the console and shell for performing mailbox moves; for the most part it comes down to which one you are most comfortable with.

A.   CREATING MOVE REQUESTS WITH THE EXCHANGE MANAGEMENT CONSOLE

During the pilot migration it was demonstrated how to initiate mailbox moves requests using the Exchange Management Console.

When it comes to the production migrations you can use filters to make the task of selecting mailboxes to be moved simpler.

1. Open the **Exchange Management Console** and navigate to **Recipient Configuration/Mailbox.**
2. Click on **Create Filter** at the top of the console.
3. Filters can be created for a number of different user attributes, such as department, the current server they are on, or by name.
4. For example, if you are batching mailbox migrations by surname you can create a filter to only show mailbox users whose surname starts with a given letter.
5. Click on **Apply Filter** to see the resulting view.

Filtering the views in this way can make it very easy to select the mailboxes that you wish to create move requests for. The **New Local Move Request** wizard is then launched from the Actions pane, and you can initiate the migration as you did earlier with the pilot group.

B.   CREATING MOVE REQUESTS WITH THE EXCHANGE MANAGEMENT SHELL

In a similar way to the Exchange Management Console the Exchange Management Shell allows filtering of mailboxes in the organization by various criteria.
For example to get the same filtered list of mailbox users with surnames starting with the letter A the following command is used:

```
[PS] C:\>Get-Recipient | Where {$_.LastName -like "A*"}
Name RecipientType
---- -------------
AAA.BBB UserMailbox
ACC.DDD UserMailbox
AEE.FFF UserMailbox
AGG.HHH UserMailbox
AII.JJJ UserMailbox
```

This output can then be piped into the New-MoveRequest command to create the move requests.
In this example the mailboxes with surnames starting with "A" are captured into an array named $surnames_a. This array is then piped into the New-MoveRequest cmdlet.

```
[PS] C:\>$surnames_a = Get-Recipient | Where {$_.LastName -like "A*"}

[PS] C:\>$surnames_a | New-MoveRequest -TargetDatabase MB-HE-01 -BatchName "Surnames_A" -
SuspendWhenReadyToComplete
```

Notice the parameters that have been used in the command above.
-TargetDatabase was used to specify which mailbox database to move the mailboxes to. If this parameter was not included the mailboxes would automatically be distributed evenly across all available mailbox databases in the AD site where the command was executed.

-BatchName was used to specify an identifier that can be used later as a search string to query those move requests.

-SuspendWhenReadyToComplete has the same effect as the check box used earlier in the pilot mailbox migrations.

Use the **Get-MoveRequest cmdlet** to check the status of the move requests.

```
[PS] C:\>Get-MoveRequest -BatchName "Surnames_A"
DisplayName Status TargetDatabase
----------- ------ --------------
AAA BBB AutoSuspended MB-HE-01
ACC DDD AutoSuspended MB-HE-01
AEE FFF AutoSuspended MB-HE-01
AGG HHH AutoSuspended MB-HE-01
AII JJJ AutoSuspended MB-HE-01
```

When they are all in a state of "AutoSuspended" you can complete the move requests by running this command.

```
[PS] C:\>Get-MoveRequest -BatchName "Surnames_A" | Resume-MoveRequest
```

The move requests will begin processing to completion.

```
[PS] C:\>Get-MoveRequest -BatchName "Surnames_A"
DisplayName Status TargetDatabase
----------- ------ --------------
AAA BBB Completed MB-HE-01
ACC DDD Completed MB-HE-01
AEE FFF Completed MB-HE-01
AGG HHH Completed MB-HE-01
AII JJJ Completed MB-HE-01
```

As another example let's look at the automatic mailbox distribution mentioned earlier. First, we'll look at how many mailboxes are on each of the mailbox databases at the moment.

```
[PS] C:\>Get-Mailbox | Group-Object -Property:Database | Select-Object name,count
Name Count
---- -----
MB-HE-01 22
ho-ex2007-mb1\First Storage Group\Mailbox Database 331
ho-ex2007-mb1\Second Storage Group\Mailbox Database 36
BR-EX2007-MB\First Storage Group\Mailbox Database 8
MB-BR-01 1
```

As you can see there are 22 mailboxes already on MB-HO-01, and 367 still on the server HO-EX2007-MB1 that are yet to be migrated.
The mailboxes on HO-EX2007-MB1 are collected into an array.

```
[PS] C:\>$headoffice = Get-Mailbox | where {$_.servername -eq "ho-ex2007-mb1"}
[PS] C:\>$headoffice.Count 367
```

From an Exchange 2010 Client Access server in the Head Office AD site the following command will create move requests for the Head Office mailboxes still on HO-EX2007-MB1, and because the – TargetDatabase parameters is omitted it will distribute them evenly across the available database in the Head Office AD site.

```
[PS] C:\>$headoffice | New-MoveRequest -BatchName "HeadOffice"
-SuspendWhenReadyToComplete
```

When the move requests have all been created, without having to wait for them to complete, we can already see the roughly even distribution across the available databases.

```
[PS] C:\>Get-MoveRequest -BatchName "HeadOffice" | group-object -property:targetdatabase |
select-object name,count
Name Count
---- -----
MB-HE-03 120
MB-HE-02 129
MB-HE-01 118
```

Production mailbox migrations may take several days or weeks depending on the size and number of mailboxes in your organization. During this phase of the project you may wish to focus solely on migrating mailboxes and providing any post-migration support for end user questions or problems that arise.

However if you do feel that you can comfortably fit more project tasks in you can also perform the public folder migration tasks described in the next section.

As a final word on mailbox move requests, each move request remains visible in the Exchange Management Console or Exchange Management Shell until it is cleared by an administrator.

You do not need to rush to clear them, however you cannot move a mailbox again when it still has a move request (even a completed one) attached to it.

MOVING PUBLIC FOLDER REPLICAS

For most organizations migrating public folders is as simple as moving replicas from one server to another. In this example scenario the public folders hosted on the Head Office Exchange 2007 server are being moved to the Head Office Exchange 2010 Mailbox server that was configured with a public folder database.

Public folder replicas are moved using the Exchange Management Shell. In this example the public folders hosted on the Branch Office Exchange 2007 Mailbox server will be moved to the Branch Office Exchange 2010 Mailbox server.

On the Exchange 2010 server open the **Exchange Management Shell**.

Microsoft has supplied a PowerShell script called **MoveAllReplicas.ps1** for moving public folder replicas.

Run the script with the following parameters:

-Server is the name of the source Exchange 2007 server
-NewServer is the name of the target Exchange 2010 server

Before running the script we can see how many folders have replicas stored on the Branch Office Exchange 2007 server.

```
[PS] C:\>Get-PublicFolder \ -Recurse | where {$_.Replicas -like "*br-ex2007-mb*"}
Name Parent Path
---- -----------
All Staff \
Branch Office \
Head Office \
```

Navigate to the scripts folder of the Exchange installation folder.

```
[PS] C:\>cd $env:exchangeinstallpath\scripts
```

Note that this is a single-line command run from the folder containing the scripts.

```
[PS] C:\Program Files\Microsoft\Exchange Server\V14\scripts>.\MoveAllReplicas.ps1 -Server BR-
EX2007-MB -NewServer BR-2K10-MB
```

When the move has completed the same command used earlier will show that the Exchange 2007 server hosts no public folder replicas, and the Exchange 2010 server does.

Note that you will need to query for the name of the Exchange 2010 public folder database name itself, not the server that hosts it.

```
[PS] C:\>Get-PublicFolder \ -Recurse | where {$_.Replicas -like "*br-ex2007-mb*"}
[PS] C:\>Get-PublicFolder \ -Recurse | where {$_.Replicas -like "*pf-br-01*"}
Name Parent Path
---- -----------
All Staff \
Branch Office \
Head Office \
```

Repeat the same process for moving replicas from any other public folder servers in your environment.

CHECKPOST – 3 Check before proceeding

Before proceeding further with your Exchange Server 2010 project, ensure that you have:

- ✓ Migrated Client Access services to Exchange Server 2010.
- ✓ Migrated email routing to Exchange Server 2010.
- ✓ Performed a pilot mailbox migration.
- ✓ Migrated all mailboxes to Exchange Server 2010.
- ✓ Migrated public folder replicas to Exchange Server 2010.

Tip: You may wish to leave the Exchange environment unchanged for a short period after completing the migrations, before you begin decommissioning Exchange 2007 servers, in case you encounter any issues that require a rollback of any services or data. This is particularly true in smaller environments where the migration may occur in a very short space of time. Larger environments are more likely to discover and resolve any issues as they progress through the migration process over several weeks.

REMOVING THE EXCHANGE 2007 SERVERS

The process of removing the Exchange 2007 servers from the organization follows a staged approach that is designed to verify that minimal or no impact will be caused by the removal of the servers, and then gradually shutting down services until the server is finally ready to be uninstalled.

PERFORMING A FINAL BACKUP OF EXCHANGE 2007 SERVERS

Before proceeding with any changes or removal of Exchange 2007 servers it is recommended to perform a final backup of each server.
You may wish to back them up to media that you can keep for a long period of time in case of the need to recover any information from the final state they were in before removal.

MOVING OFFLINE ADDRESS BOOKS

The Offline Address Book generation role needs to be moved to an Exchange Server 2010 Mailbox server.

1. On an Exchange 2010 server launch the **Exchange Management Console** and navigate to **Organization Configuration/Mailbox**.
2. On the **Offline Address Book** tab right-click the Offline Address Book and choose **Move**.
3. In the Move Offline Address Book wizard click on **Browse**.
4. Choose the Exchange Server 2010 Mailbox server to be the new OAB generation server. Click **OK** and then click **Move** to continue.
5. A warning message may appear regarding turning off public folder publishing for the offline address book prematurely. Public folder distribution is required if you still have Outlook 2003 clients in your environment.
6. By default OAB generation occurs at 5:00am daily. If you need to accelerate the process you can right-click the offline address book and select **Update**.
7. Do not turn off public folder distribution if you still have Outlook 2003 clients in the environment.
8. However now that the Offline Address Book has been moved you should also modify the web-based distribution for the OAB. In the **Exchange Management Console** right-click the OAB and choose **Properties**.
9. On the **Distribution** tab tick the box to **Enable web-based distribution**, and then add at least one Exchange 2010 Client Access server in each site to the list, and remove each of the Exchange 2007 servers from the list as well.
10. Click **OK** to apply the changes.

VERIFYING INTERNAL MAIL ROUTING

Before removing the Exchange 2007 Hub Transport servers we want to be sure that no further applications or devices are relaying mail through the servers.

Earlier we enabled protocol logging to allow the log files to be inspected for any remaining SMTP relay traffic. If you didn't do this earlier then you can enable protocol logging now and wait a few days to see if any traffic is logged.

The files can be found in the Exchange installation path, which by default is **C:\Program Files\Microsoft\Exchange Server\TransportRoles\Logs\ProtocolLog\SmtpReceive**.

A typical SMTP session will generate more than one line of logging, so this means potentially hundreds or thousands of lines of logging, maybe over multiple log files, which need to be consolidated down into a list of unique IP addresses.

This consolidation is made easy thanks to Logparser which can be downloaded and installed from http://www.microsoft.com/downloads/details.aspx?FamilyID=890cd06b-abf8-4c25-91b2-f8d975cf8c07&displaylang=en on the Hub Transport server, and then launch it from the Start Menu.

A very simple query to extract the unique IP addresses from the SMTP log files looks like this. This is a single-line command run from the Logparser program directory.

```
C:\Program Files (x86)\Log Parser 2.2>logparser -i:CSV "SELECT DISTINCT EXTRACT_
PREFIX(remote-endpoint,0,':') FROM 'C:\Program Files\Microsoft\Exchange Server\T
ransportRoles\Logs\ProtocolLog\SmtpReceive\*.log'" -nSkipLines:4
EXTRACT_PREFIX(remote-endpoint, 0, ':')
---------------------------------------
10.1.1.27
Statistics:
-----------
Elements processed: 16
Elements output: 1
Execution time: 0.00 seconds
```

You have now got a nice short list of the unique IP addresses that are using the server for SMTP communications and can go and investigate the applications or device configurations that are causing it, before you shut down the Exchange 2007 Hub Transport servers for good.

VERIFYING COMPLETE MAILBOX MIGRATION

Depending on the size of your organization and the team of administrators who manage the environment it is possible that new mailboxes may have been created on the Exchange 2007 servers after the mailbox migrations were completed.

You can verify that no mailbox users exist on the Exchange 2007 servers by running the following commands from the Exchange Management Shell on an Exchange 2010 server.

```
[PS] C:\>Set-ADServerSettings -ViewEntireForest 1
[PS] C:\>$2007mbservers = Get-ExchangeServer | where {$_.AdminDisplayVersion -like "*Version
8.*" -AND $_.IsMailboxServer -eq "True"}
[PS] C:\>$2007mbservers | Get-Mailbox
```

Note the use of Set-ADServerSettings to change the recipient scope to the entire forest. This is important for multi-domain organizations, because the Exchange 2007 uninstall process does not always correctly detect the existence of remaining mailboxes on the server if the mailbox user is in a different domain in the forest, which can lead to data loss.

If the last command returns no results then there should be no more Exchange 2007 mailboxes in the organization.

REMOVING EXCHANGE 2007 MAILBOX AND PUBLIC FOLDER DATABASES

Before removing any databases from Exchange 2007 servers it is recommended to first dismount them for a period of time to determine whether any negative impact occurs when they are unavailable.

A.   DISMOUNTING MAILBOX AND PUBLIC FOLDER DATABASES

1. On an Exchange 2007 server open the Exchange Management Console and navigate to **Server Configuration/Mailbox**.
2. Select a mailbox server and then right-click each database and choose **Dismount Database**.

Repeat this process for each mailbox and public folder database on the Exchange 2007 servers, then perform some testing or simply wait to see if any negative impact occurs.

B.   DELETING MAILBOX AND PUBLIC FOLDER DATABASES

When you are satisfied that having the databases unavailable does not cause any negative impact for your organization you can proceed with removal of the databases.

1. On an Exchange 2007 server launch the Exchange Management Console, right-click the databases and choose **Remove**.
2. You will be asked to confirm the deletion. After you have removed the database the files themselves are left on the disk as a precaution in case you need to reconnect the database again.
3. You can leave the storage groups themselves in place so that the Information Store service can still start properly if the server is rebooted for any reason.
4. When deleting a public folder database the database must be mounted first before the server will allow it to be deleted.
5. In some cases the public folder database may still contain replicas for system folders.

Before you spend too much time trying to solve this issue, first try leaving it alone for a day or two. Sometimes the public folder replication takes 24-48 hours to finish processing all the changes, even when it appears to be complete.

If you're still unable to remove a public folder database then a useful tool for hunting down the last remaining folder replicas is PFDAVAdmin32 from Microsoft.

The tool is available for download at:
http://www.microsoft.com/download/en/details.aspx?displaylang=en&id=22427

Because PFDAVAdmin requires DotNET Framework 1.1, its **recommend you install it on** a workstation instead of your Exchange servers.

When you launch PFDAVAdmin connect to the public folder server you are trying to remove, and once the folder list finishes loading you can begin looking for folders that still have replicas on that server.

One of the fastest ways to do this is to run the **Export Replica Lists** task from the **Tools** menu of PFDAVAdmin, and then simply search through the text file that it creates.

If you are still unable to remove the public folder **database you can use ADSIEdit** to remove it instead.

This method should only be used if you are sure that all content has replicated from the public database.

1. Click on the Start Menu and select **Run**, then launch "**adsiedit.msc**".
2. Right-click the root of the console and choose **Connect to…**
3. Choose the naming context of Configuration and click **OK** to connect.
4. Navigate to **CN=Services/CN=Microsoft Exchange/CN=<Your Organization Name>/CN=Administrative Groups/CN=Exchange Administrative Group (FYDIBOHF23SPDLT)/CN=Servers/CN=<Your Exchange 2007 Server Name>/CN=Information Store/CN=<Storage Group Name>**.
5. Right-click the public folder database that you want to remove and choose **Delete.**
6. Repeat the same process for any other Exchange 2007 public folder databases you want to remove.

UNINSTALLING EXCHANGE SERVER 2007

When all data and services have been migrated to Exchange 2010 you can remove the Exchange 2007 servers from the organization.
The following order is recommended for removing the old servers:
1. Mailbox (including public folder servers)
2. Client Access
3. Hub Transport

For clustered mailbox servers remove the passive node first, followed by the active node.

If you are running a Single Copy Cluster refer to the following TechNet Article Numbers for some additional considerations:-

bb885058 – Most Important

Exchange Server 2007 can be removed from servers using **Programs and Features** in the **Control Panel** (also known as Add/Remove Programs depending on the version of Windows Server you're running). Highlight Exchange 2007 in the list of installed programs and click **Uninstall**.

When Exchange Maintenance Mode launches click **Next** to continue.
Uncheck the boxes for any server roles that are installed on the server, as well as for the management tools. Click **Next** to continue.
Exchange setup will perform a readiness check to verify that the server is ready for removal. If no remaining dependencies are found the check will pass and you can click **Uninstall** to begin.
When the uninstall process has completed click **Finish**.
You can now continue with your normal server decommissioning process to remove the base server itself, if they perform no other role within your environment.

UPGRADING DISTRIBUTION GROUPS

With all of the Exchange 2007 servers removed from the organization the final task is to update the distribution groups in the organization to Exchange 2010.
This is not a mandatory step, however if you do not complete it you will not be able to take advantage of new features in Exchange 2010 such as moderated transport. They will appear greyed out in the properties of distribution groups.
To upgrade all distribution groups to Exchange 2010 use the Exchange Management Shell to run the following command.

```
[PS] C:\>Get-DistributionGroup | Set-DistributionGroup -ForceUpgrade
```

ALL DONE – Phew! Was it really hard with this document – do send your comments to me.

Oh! There is one thing I would suggest ....

RUN AN EXCHANGE BEST PRACTICES ANALYZER SCAN

After performing so many changes to your production environment it is recommended to run another Exchange Best Practices Analyzer scan to check for any issues that may have arisen.
The Best Practices Analyzer can be launched from the **Toolbox** section of the Exchange Management Console.

And ... Take a Full Windows Backup with VSS Enabled.